Greece & Rome

NEW SURVEYS IN THE CLASSICS No. 45

THE SOPHISTS

BY

MAURO BONAZZI

Published for the Classical Association

CAMBRIDGE UNIVERSITY PRESS

2020

Shaftesbury Road, Cambridge CB2 8EA, United Kingdom

One Liberty Plaza, 20th Floor, New York, NY 10006, USA

477 Williamstown Road, Port Melbourne, VIC 3207, Australia

314–321, 3rd Floor, Plot 3, Splendor Forum, Jasola District Centre, New Delhi – 110025, India

103 Penang Road, #05–06/07, Visioncrest Commercial, Singapore 238467

Cambridge University Press is part of Cambridge University Press & Assessment, a department of the University of Cambridge.

We share the University's mission to contribute to society through the pursuit of education, learning and research at the highest international levels of excellence.

www.cambridge.org
Information on this title: www.cambridge.org/9781108706216

A catalogue record for this publication is available from the British Library

ISBN 978-1-108-70621-6 Paperback

To FERNANDA DECLEVA CAIZZI
IL MIGLIOR FABBRO

CONTENTS

FOREWORD: A NOTE ON THE QUOTATION OF FRAGMENTS AND TESTIMONIES PERTAINING TO THE SOPHISTS

Probably as a consequence of the negative judgement which often weighed against them – yet not unlike the case for many other ancient writers – almost no complete texts by the sophists survive: we must rely on quotes and testimonies. Although recently discovered papyri have broadened our knowledge, to this day the essential edition of the works of the sophists – and Presocratic philosophers more generally – is Hermann Diels's *Die Fragmente der Vorsokratiker*, later revised and corrected by Walter Kranz (Diels and Kranz 1951–2, henceforth D.-K.). This collection is in three volumes: the first two contain all the sources, arranged in ninety chapters (each chapter usually corresponding to an author), while the third volume features a word index and a selective index of names and passages. The section on the sophists coincides with Chapters 79–90 of the second volume. For each author, the chapters are divided into 'testimonies' and 'fragments', which are respectively marked with the letters A and B (this subdivision is not adopted in all cases, but only when the number of passages allows it – this is not the case, for instance, with Xeniades, Lycophron, and the *Dissoi logoi*); in some cases we also find a third section, C, containing 'imitations'. Thus 80B3 will stand for fragment 3 of Protagoras, while 87A6 will stand for testimony 6 on Antiphon, and so on (the same criteria generally apply to all other Presocratic philosophers as well).

Though yet unsurpassed, *Die Vorsokratiker* can now be fruitfully complemented with a new impressive collection of testimonies and fragments: André Laks and Glenn W. Most, *Early Greek Philosophy*, published in 2016 in the Loeb Classical Library (and in French by Fayard with the title *Les débuts de la philosophie. Des premiers penseurs grecs à Socrate*, henceforth L.-M.). The sophists are presented in the eighth and ninth volumes, sections 31–42. Each chapter normally comprises three sections, with each entry being identified by a number preceded by a letter: P indicates information on the life, character, and sayings of a given philosopher; D the doctrines; R the reception of their thought and writings. Unless not otherwise noted, all translations of the sophists are based on Laks and Most's translations. Other useful translations are Freeman 1948, Kent Sprague 1972, and Dillon and Gergel 2003. With regard to Plato and Aristotle, our two most important testimonies regarding the sophists, the translations are taken from Cooper 1997 and Barnes 1984, respectively. For all the other authors, the translations are from the Loeb Classical Texts (with minor changes).

This book, a revised and updated version of my previous book, *I sofisti* (Rome, 2010), would never have seen the light without the support and the competence of the editor of the New Surveys series, Phillip Horky. My warmest thanks are due to him, and also to Sergio Knipe for his help with the translation.

I THE SOPHISTS: HISTORY OF A NAME AND PREJUDICE

One day around the year 430 BC, before dawn, a young and promising Athenian, Hippocrates, son of Apollodorus, hastens to Socrates' house to rouse him from his sleep. The reason for this bizarre behaviour soon becomes clear: Protagoras is in Athens! With a knowing smile, Socrates answers that he is already aware of this, as though he could not really understand the reason for all this excitement. But Hippocrates shows no hesitation: Protagoras, the great sophist, he who 'makes people wise', is in Athens – an opportunity not to be missed! The two of them must leave immediately, and Socrates must help Hippocrates gain access to Callias' house, where the sophist is staying. However, Socrates insists on enquiring about the reason for Hippocrates' excitement: does he wish to become a sophist?

> 'And if somebody asks you what do you expect to become in going to Protagoras?'
>
> He blushed in response – there was just enough daylight now to show him up – and said, 'If this is all like the previous cases, then, obviously, to become a sophist.'
>
> 'What? You? Wouldn't you be ashamed to present yourself to the Greek world as a sophist?'
>
> 'Yes, I would, Socrates, to be perfectly honest.' (Plato, *Protagoras*, 310a–312a)

This famous page from Plato – the prologue of the *Protagoras* – probably constitutes the most compelling example of the ambiguous fame attached to the name of the sophists. That fame has not changed much over the centuries: the sophists have always been the object of violent polemics and passionate vindication. After centuries of criticism, in the modern age the sophists received the support of some most distinguished philosophers: first from Hegel, who regarded them as the masters of Greece, then from some English liberals (in particular George Grote), and finally – and even more staunchly – from Nietzsche, who saw them as the most genuine representatives of the Greek spirit.[1] Later, Popper was to go so far as to speak of a 'great generation', while other scholars have even suggested that ours is the age of the Third Sophistic.[2] At the same time, however, 'sophist' and

[1] On the importance and limits of the interpretations put forward by Hegel and English liberals, see Kerferd 1981a: 4–14; on Nietzsche, see Consigny 1994.

[2] Popper 1971: 162. One author who describes the contemporary age as a 'Third Sophistic' is Vitanza 1997; see also Fowler 2014. See too Rorty 1979: 157. The expression 'Second Sophistic' is used to describe the revival in the Imperial age of certain elements introduced by the sophists in

'sophistic' are still used to describe 'a verbal philosophy that is neither sound nor serious', to quote Lalande's *Vocabulaire technique et critique de philosophie* – almost a paraphrase of the scathing verdict of Aristotle, who had dismissed sophistry as the wisdom of appearances, and hence an appearance of wisdom (*Sophistical Refutations*, 171b34). In other words, in antiquity, just as in the modern age, the sophists elicited sympathy at times, but more often deep hostility; and neither situation has helped to adequately reconstruct their thought. In order to make an appropriate assessment, it is necessary first to clarify the topic to be discussed: the primary aim of the present book is to provide a reliable reconstruction of the sophists' thought – as far as the sources allow it – within their historical and philosophical context. It will then be up to the reader to assess their importance.

Who were the sophists?

In order to adequately analyse the sophists' thought, it is necessary to address a highly challenging preliminary problem: to identify which thinkers can legitimately be called 'sophists', and to clarify what distinguishes them from other intellectuals of their age. One often speaks of the 'sophistic' as though its definition was taken for granted, as though it were clear to everyone in antiquity. Yet, when taken literally, even the term 'sophistic' itself is improper and misleading, insofar as in fifth-century Greece there was never a homogeneous tradition of thought or institutionalized school to which the label 'sophistic' could be applied.[3] In the ancient sources, the term from which our word 'sophist' derives, *sophistês*, expresses a much more fluid situation, encompassing a more or less extensive range of meanings: *sophistês* is used for a poet like Homer, a politician like Solon, and a mythical figure like Prometheus. According to Plato, a sophist is 'troublesome and hard to grasp' and there is a risk that each person will assign a different meaning to the word (*Sophist*, 218b–d). Such a broad use of the word

the fifth century BC. The focus in this case was on rhetorical and literary themes, while the more strictly philosophical aspect was largely overlooked. For this reason, I will not be discussing the phenomenon here (for an interesting attempt to link the fifth-century sophistic and the Second Sophistic, see Cassin 1995).

[3] It may be worth noting that, in the surviving testimonies, the only sophist to describe himself as such is Protagoras in the Platonic dialogue that bears his name (*Protagoras*, 317b = 80A5 D.-K. = 31P13a L.-M.).

risks making it useless, as it would come to generically describe anyone who has some relationship with knowledge or wisdom (*sophia* in Greek).

Fortunately, however, a more precise definition can be found. While the ancients were quite aware that the 'sophistic' was not a homogeneous school of thought, they acknowledged the sophists as a group of thinkers who, over the course of the fifth century, had promoted a radical renewal of the Greek cultural tradition. This makes it possible to narrow down the scope of the term: while doubts may be raised about this or that figure, it is possible to identify a core of thinkers who may be regarded as part of this 'movement' (to quote George Kerferd, the author of a key study on the sophists).[4] In this respect, the most authoritative contribution comes from Hermann Diels, who devoted the final section of his extensive edition of the Presocratics to 'ancient sophistic', by including testimonies and fragments pertaining to nine authors and two anonymous treatises: Protagoras, Xeniades, Gorgias, Lycophron, Prodicus, Hippias, Thrasymachus, Antiphon, and Critias, to which we should add the so-called Anonymus Iamblichi or the 'Anonymous of Iamblichus', the author of a text preserved by the Neoplatonist philosopher Iamblichus (third–fourth century CE), and the anonymous author of the *Dissoi logoi*, a set of dialectical exercises concerning standard topics for argumentation. Diels hesitated at first about including the sophists in his work; nonetheless, the sources he selected – with some possible integrations (for example, Alcidamas and figures such as Polus, Euthydemus, and Dionysodorus, who are only known to us through the little information that Plato provides) – make up the ranks of the 'sophists', for us as much as for the ancients.[5]

This point can be agreed upon. But what criteria allow us to better define the sophists? One hint comes from the very meaning of the term *sophistês* and from the history of its use: by briefly retracing this

[4] Kerferd 1981a.

[5] Naturally, this list, while perfectly reasonable, is not decisive. To give just one example of how difficult it is to precisely identify the sophists: in his writings, Aristotle applies this label to four authors alone, namely Lycophron, Polyeidos, Bryson, and Aristippus. Only the first of these is reckoned among the sophists today (Polyeidos appears to have been a poet and literary critic, while Bryson and Aristippus are possibly to be associated with the milieu of the Socratic schools). All four are called sophists in relation to language and ethico-political issues, which – as we shall see – constituted the privileged object of reflection for the sophists.

history, we can identify some key features.[6] Other clues may then be inferred through an engagement with the ancient sources. The word *sophistês* is based on the root **soph-*, which we also find in *sophos* (knowledgeable, wise) and *sophia* (knowledge, wisdom), two terms commonly used from early Greece to express the notion of *skill* in some field or craft. Starting from this general meaning, *sophos* gradually came to describe individuals who were knowledgeable and accomplished in intellectual pursuits. These 'wise men' (*sophoi* in the plural), usually poets or soothsayers, possessed a kind of knowledge that was unattainable by other men and which could have beneficial effects. From the fifth century BC onwards, *sophistês* entered into use as a synonym of *sophos*: to be more precise, *sophistês* is formed from the verb *sophizesthai*, which is to say 'to exercise *sophia*'. A 'sophist', therefore, is someone who acts as a *sophos*, someone who possesses intellectual knowledge either in a general sense or in a specific discipline. *Sophistês*, originally a synonym of *sophos*, thus came to describe something more narrow, something more suited to the needs of an increasingly sophisticated society: the exercise of knowledge in practice is teaching, as a profession; hence, a sophist is a teacher, and educator. This is an initial defining feature, from which others follow.

The professionalizing of the sophist's role helps to explain another crucial characteristic that further distinguishes his social position, namely his salary. Insofar as the sophist imparts some teachings, he expects some payment in return – a request that is only natural for us, but which was very unusual for the ancient Greeks, who regarded the idea of teaching wisdom or virtue to anyone for a fee as something quite shocking.[7] Secondly, what also distinguishes the activity of the sophist – albeit to a lesser degree than the demand for pay – is his itinerant character. The sophists are teachers who share their knowledge in exchange for a fee in the many cities they visit. This is hardly surprising, given that almost all sophists were born far away from the major cultural

[6] On the meaning of *sophistês* and its history, see the following analyses: Untersteiner 1949–62: i.xvi–xxiii; Guthrie 1971: 27–35; and Kerferd 1981a: 24–41. An alternative reconstruction is put forward by Edmunds 2006, according to whom *sophistês* only entered into use as a technical term in the fourth century BC, whereas in the fifth it described a gamut of intellectual figures, including soothsayers, dithyrambic poets, scientists, and orators. This study confirms the importance played by Plato and Aristotle in the definition of the sophists' identity; still, it does not rule out that by the fifth century the term 'sophist' had already come to be associated with the practice of teaching, which is perhaps the most distinguishing feature of the sophists' activity; on this, see also Tell 2011.

[7] Blank 1985.

and political centres of their day, such as Athens: travelling for them was practically a requirement.[8] The itinerant character of the sophists' teaching may seem like a trivial fact, but actually has some important implications – as we shall see – that at least partly account for the degree of hostility they incurred.

These three criteria (teaching, the charging of a fee, and travel) allow us to narrow down the field of our enquiry, insofar as they help us distinguish a 'sophist' such as Protagoras from a 'sophist' such as Prometheus. Protagoras was a teacher who visited many cities of the Greek world, exercising his profession for a fee; by contrast, when Aeschylus calls Prometheus a sophist, he is only highlighting his knowledge and commitment to help people (*Prometheus Bound*, 944). What is even more interesting is the case of Solon, who had also travelled the known world: Herodotus (1.29) calls him both *sophistês* and *philosophos*, not because he wishes to portray him as a forerunner of the sophists and philosophers, but to praise his desire for knowledge (the literal meaning of *philo-sophia* being 'love of wisdom') and the experience he had acquired through his travels – two virtues which are certainly noteworthy, but which do not distinguish the sophists' teaching activity.

Polemicists, bad teachers, and fake philosophers: the charges against the sophists

Based on the three criteria just outlined, it is possible to identify a group of 'sophists' in the sense in which Hermann Diels and all modern scholars have understood this term. Still, difficulties remain. Thus far, the sophists appear to resemble one another in terms of their practical activities, without having any shared status. But if this is the case, how do the sophists differ from all other teachers and educators? Once again, the ancient sources are ambiguous on the matter, and the simplest answer seems to be that there is no difference between the sophists and other teachers: in a way, all teachers are sophists.

[8] To get an idea of the extent of the sophists' travels, see the profiles in Appendix 1. It is important to bear in mind that many sophists also travelled for political reasons, acting as ambassadors of their cities: see esp. Plato, *Hippias*, 282b–c, on Gorgias, Prodicus, and Hippias. One may recall Gorgias' famous embassy to Athens in 427 BC. Similar embassies have been suggested in relation to Thrasymachus, albeit on less certain grounds: see White 1995 and Yunis 1997. It is also worth mentioning Antiphon's famous embassy to Sparta after the coup of 411 BC – assuming that the hypothesis that identifies the sophist with the orator by that name is correct.

Curiously enough, this is the position of Plato's Protagoras in a passage of the dialogue that bears his name, where he mentions teachers of gymnastics and music, along with poets and prophets, as the forerunners of the 'sophist's art' (Plato, *Protagoras*, 316c–317d, partly quoted by Diels-Kranz as testimony 80A5 D.-K. = Soph. R11 L.-M.). However, this very passage shows that the situation is rather more complex: Protagoras admits that the profession of the sophist is very dangerous, as it 'stirs considerable hostility, enmities and intrigues', to the point that sophists often even risk coming across as swindlers; and it is precisely in order to avoid this hostility that Protagoras associates himself with universally esteemed figures such as the poets Homer, Hesiod, and Simonides. Protagoras' move is a brilliant and shrewd one, but clearly it does not reflect his contemporaries' beliefs: there are more differences than affinities between Homer and the sophists, as well as between teachers of gymnastics or music and the sophists. While affinities lie in the common practice of teaching, the divergences can be identified in the things taught and the teaching strategies.

At the present state of our knowledge, it is not easy to establish the exact nature of these divergences – and not merely because few reliable testimonies are available. One equally important aspect, which cannot be overlooked, is the fact that the subject taught varied from sophist to sophist: Protagoras focused on politics, but some sophists – including Hippias – also dealt with other disciplines ('arithmetic, astronomy, geometry, music, and poetry': Plato, *Protagoras*, 318d–e), whereas Gorgias' only concern was to make people clever at speaking, 'to train skilled orators' (82A21 D.-K. = 32D47 L.-M.). At first sight, then, it would seem almost impossible to find any guiding thread in the sophists' activity. Upon closer inspection, however, this is not really the case: if not in positive terms, the sophists at least agree from a negative standpoint, in terms of their polemical aim. And this, when examined in the light of their opponents' responses, can help us more accurately define the sophists' activities.

One aspect that constantly emerges from the surviving testimonies is the fact that the sophists' teaching – whatever its object – entailed a staunch opposition to traditional forms of teaching (such as music and gymnastics) and even more so to other types of knowledge: the sophists not only upheld the worth of their new intellectual teaching against traditional education, but even boasted that they were capable of refuting poets and philosophers, physicians and mathematicians, and more generally the experts in all other disciplines.[9] As has often been noted, competition plays a central role in ancient Greece, a society lacking 'official' types of authority: each teacher was required to provide concrete proof of his superiority over other aspiring 'wise men'.[10] The sophists offer a striking example of this polemical spirit. Their teaching constitutes a remarkable challenge to the claims to truth made by other experts in the *polis*, and betrays the sophists' desire to establish themselves as the new intellectual masters in Greece.[11]

From the point of view of their opponents, the sophists' claim to be capable of taking the place of experts amounted to the promotion of a strictly verbal kind of knowledge: the sophists do not really know what they are talking about; they are only brilliant speakers who conceal their shortcomings behind linguistic tricks; their only concern is how to win an argument. Accusations of this sort may be found in many texts by Hippocratic physicians, who label the sophists 'professional defamers' (see Appendix 2). No less eloquent are Aristotle's observations, which convey a further and more serious criticism. Aristotle is less drastic than other detractors and grants the sophists a few merits: it is true – he states – that the sophists have chiefly focused on language and argumentative techniques; yet their analyses are still worth discussing, if only to highlight their errors and fallacies. In Aristotle's perspective, however, the real problem is this: the sophists' exclusive interest in language implies that they do not examine reality, causes, and principles, which is to say that they are not genuine philosophers at all. At best they are dialecticians, grammarians, and orators, even though it is tempting

[9] See Fait 2007: xl–xliv.

[10] Lloyd 1979.

[11] The sophists' ambition explains why their activity entailed not only private lessons but also public performances (*epideixis*): see Guthrie 1971: 41–4. Privately, the teacher was chiefly concerned with presenting certain argumentative schemes that the pupil could then make use of for his own benefit (see Natali 1986; it is possible that these arguments were subsequently brought together to form genuine discourses that might serve as a model for students). Public performance was a privileged avenue for sophists to promote themselves and their wisdom even before an extensive audience (for instance, during solemn celebrations such as the Olympic Games). For a vivid description of these performances, see Lloyd 1987: 79–102; for analyses of the possible circulation of these discourses in written form, see O'Sullivan 1996 and Thomas 2003. While bearing this distinction in mind, we should not overemphasize the break between public and private, since even the teaching of arguments could take place in open contexts: this is the case, for instance, in Plato's *Euthydemus*, where Euthydemus and Dionysodorus, mocking their interlocutors, present argumentative schemes that their pupils can apply to new cases. The truly enduring feature of the sophists' activity is its agonistic-competitive character. Interesting points on the historical and cultural context may also be found in Soverini 1998.

to simply dismiss them as word-jugglers who stand out for their (unfounded) claim to master the art of discourse.[12]

Insofar as sophistic teaching was simply reduced to a verbal argument, it is easy to understand why the sophists were also accused of being bad teachers, or teachers of immorality: exclusively concerned with winning arguments, the sophists proved incapable of tackling the great moral questions that lie at the basis of any real education. In fact, the importance of this accusation also depended on the social problems associated with the itinerant character of the sophists' activity. Particularly in archaic societies, education was a means to hand down values and beliefs from father to son, a social mechanism intended to ensure order and continuity.[13] With the sophists, this circle was broken: their social otherness ensured their independence with respect to the various communities in which they found themselves teaching. As foreigners and outsiders in the cities hosting them, they felt free to question everything and to scrutinize what were traditionally perceived as absolute, unchangeable, and undeniable values. With the sophists, the idea that cultural traditions are relative gained ground, as people realized that the values of a society are not absolute, but are rather the historical product of such a society. If we add the fact that the sophists often favoured provocation and paradox for 'promotional' reasons, as a means to attract potential clients, it is easy to understand why within a short time they were made the target of the predictable and banal accusation of subverting all values. Thus in the *Clouds*, written by the great comic poet Aristophanes and first performed in 423 BC, the sophists are presented as unscrupulous, hypocritical, quibbling charlatans (see lines 441–51): they are masters of the 'worse discourse',

[12] Significantly, in the first book of the *Metaphysics*, the treatise that is usually regarded as the first history of philosophy, no mention is made of the sophists, whereas their theses are widely discussed in the treatises of the *Organon* – in particular, in the *Sophistical Refutations*. On Aristotle and the sophists, see the observations made by Classen 1981, who notes that, although Aristotle does not regard the sophists as genuine philosophers, he does not simply despise them either. Aristotle's interpretation was especially influential among the great Latin orators, from Cicero to Quintilian, who only dealt with the sophists in relation to their rhetorical studies. Among modern scholars, a similar interpretation has been upheld by Gomperz 1912 and, more recently, in a completely different context, by several American scholars interested in a reassessment of rhetoric (see e.g. Schiappa 1991 on Protagoras and Consigny 2001 on Gorgias). Along much the same lines, Michael Gagarin, who is the author of some of the most enlightening contributions on the ancient sophists, has stressed the central importance of *logos* (which can mean 'word', 'speech', or 'reason') as the cornerstone of the sophists' investigations (see, for example, Gagarin 2002 and 2008). While the importance assigned to *logos* is indisputable, it does not imply a lack of interest in ethical and political issues, as we shall see.

[13] Goldhill 1986: 222–7.

the discourse which with unjust arguments overturns the better discourse and contradicts the laws in such a way as to make injustice triumph (lines 882–4).[14] Naturally, their teaching is not an innocuous abstraction, but has concrete effects, which affect society to its very core – or, rather, subvert it: Aristophanes' comedy ends with a son beating his father, a gesture which constitutes the most eloquent evidence of the overturning of traditional values.[15] The sophists are represented as the bad teachers of Athens (and the whole of Greece), those responsible for its moral and political crisis.

I will assess the soundness of these charges at different stages in the course of the present investigation, in order expose their limits and prejudiced character. For the moment, I only wish to note that both accusations in a way depend on what may be regarded as the sophists' most important contribution: their acknowledgement of the fact that reality is 'problematic'.[16] It is this awareness which leads the sophists to investigate new issues and to question established values, as was already observed by Plato himself – the sophists' fiercest opponent in a way, but also the philosopher who had most clearly grasped the philosophical and political significance of the challenge they posed.[17] This not only acquits the sophists of the charge of promoting immorality, but assigns them a prominent place in the history of philosophy – a point I will be discussing at length in the following chapters.[18] For the time being, it is important to note that these two accusations allow us to better define the primary aim of the sophists' research and teaching: the charge of playing with words may be explained by considering the sophists' utmost interest in the issue of language, while the accusation of promoting immorality is due to their interest in practical, ethical, and political problems. The sophists' favourite object of enquiry was the art of speech (*logos*), and in particular its practical and political applications. Language and politics, then, are two of

[14] The thinly veiled allusion here is to Protagoras, who promised to 'make the weaker argument the stronger' (80B6b D.-K.): a provocative claim in its ambiguity, given that 'weaker' might also mean less just.

[15] Besides, the sophists had touched upon this theme too in a provocative fashion: see Antiphon 87B44B, 5.4-8 D.-K. = 37D38 L.-M.

[16] Paci 1957: 126.

[17] See now Corey 2015.

[18] Significantly enough, aside from a few exceptions, the dominant view today is precisely that the sophists' activity entailed an engagement with ontological and political issues. This may be inferred from the most authoritative studies on the subject, which, while disagreeing on many points, agree at least on this one – from Untersteiner 1954 (first published in Italian 1949) to Kerferd 1981a, from Guthrie 1971 (first published 1969) to Cassin 1995.

their chief interests. Contrary to what Aristotle suggests, research on language and arguments is not only of theoretical relevance, but also entails practical repercussions, insofar as the sophists' teaching promises to bring their pupils success in their private and public life. This – it is worth stressing once more – does not justify any 'strong' interpretation of the sophists, as members of the same 'schools': the sophists are grouped together, not because they uphold the same doctrines, but because they share the same focuses of interest (namely language and politics), the same method of investigation, and similar aims.[19] These points will suffice as an initial overview.

The reticence of the ancient sources notwithstanding, it is possible, then, to reach some general conclusions on the sophists. They were travelling teachers, who moved from city to city and taught for a fee (these being the external criteria). Their thought and teaching focused on man, his nature, and his needs. This led them to concentrate on issues pertaining to language and politics, which does not mean – as we shall see – that they ignored the more traditional topics of Presocratic reflection (such as *physis*, for instance). A link between all the various sophists is to be found in this sharing of the same problems and attitudes, rather than in the upholding of common theses (internal criteria). This accounts for the ambition of each sophist, who in polemical opposition to other sophists as much as to poets and philosophers sought to establish himself as the new intellectual master that Greece needed. Succinctly put, such is the view which a unitary presentation of the sophists supports.

The richness and complexity of the sophists' challenge is eloquently attested to by the *Dissoi logoi*, which present the sophists' aim in the following terms:

> I think that it belongs <to the same> man and to the same art to be able to discuss briefly, to know <the> truth of things, to judge a legal case correctly, to be able to make speeches to the people, to know the art of speeches, and to teach about the nature of all things, both their present condition and their origins. (90.8 D.-K. = 40.8.1 L.-M.)

No doubt, it was an ambitious aim.

[19] Gagarin 2008: 23.

II BEING AND TRUTH, HUMANITY AND REALITY

In order to understand the meaning and scope of the challenge that the sophists present to us, we must clear the field of all ambiguities and prejudices. All too often the sophist is only taken into consideration as a polemical target, as a counterpart to the philosopher: whereas the philosopher argues in order to seek the truth, the sophist only tries to win an argument; and whereas the philosopher concerns himself with problems in all of their complexity, the sophist instrumentally focuses on fashionable topics that might interest his public of potential pupils (in other words, people willing to pay him). These contrasts are repeated not only in relation to the future, which is to say to Plato and Aristotle, but also, retrospectively, in relation to the so-called 'Presocratic philosophers'. As a consequence, the sophists find themselves in a sort of no man's land, and their activities appear to mark a break in the history of philosophy, interrupting its toilsome and earnest progression from myth to reason.

Like all schematic reconstructions, the one just provided gives rise to some serious misunderstandings. One initial misunderstanding concerns the very concept of 'philosophy': up until the end of the fifth century there was no discipline of 'philosophy', possessing a distinctive epistemological status and opposed to other literary genres such as history or rhetoric. Heraclitus – to quote but one figure among those whom we regard as philosophers – uses the term to mock Pythagoras and Hesiod, accusing them of knowing many things without really understanding any at all (22B35 D.-K. = Her. 40D L.-M.). As a non-polemical term of praise, the historian Herodotus calls the poet and politician Solon a 'philosopher', commending his thirst for knowledge (1.30.2); along much the same lines, Pericles goes so far as to claim that all Athenians are philosophers (Thuc. 2.40.1). Philosophy, as we understand it, which is to say as an independent discipline, is a later invention by Plato and Aristotle: what we find in the fifth century, rather, are many prose writers (including the sophists) and poets engaging in an all-round debate that touches upon authors ranging from Homer to Parmenides, from Anaxagoras to Simonides. (It is important to remind ourselves that the same kind of openness is also displayed by Plato, Aristotle, and many other ancient philosophers.)

Only by setting out from a correct historical contextualization can we address the delicate question of the sophists' contribution to the history of ancient thought. The sophists were no doubt interested in language and all the issues related to the problem of language (argumentative techniques, rhetoric, poetry, and literary criticism), since this was the topic which most interested their public, especially in democratic Athens. However, this is not to say that they did not also deal with other 'philosophical' problems which the Presocratics had investigated and which Plato and Aristotle were to take up again – quite the contrary.

The vagueness of the concept of 'Presocratic' has often led to the misguided attempt to draw a clear-cut distinction between natural philosophers and sophists, spawning the cliché that the former only discussed nature, and the latter the human world. Like all clichés, this one contains both an element of truth and an element of falsehood. It is true that the Presocratics' investigations chiefly focused on *physis* (nature), while the sophists concerned themselves with what more specifically pertains to humanity. But it is just as true that the Presocratics made some very important contributions to the study of language and human psychology, and that the sophists also dealt with the problems of *physis* and human's relationship with the world. In other words, what changes is the perspective, not the topics discussed: the Presocratics searched for the elements of continuity between human beings and reality, while the sophists were interested in the issue of what distinguishes humankind. The change of perspective, however, does not depend on any lack of interest of the latter towards the former: it is the consequence of a critical engagement.

Ancient sources repeatedly bear witness to the sophists' interest in the Presocratics' *physis*. The most significant example is provided by Gorgias' treatise *On Nature or On Not-Being*, which from its very title sets out to overthrow the theses of Melissus and Parmenides (Gorgias, after all, was a pupil of Empedocles: see 82A3, 10 D.-K. = 32P4–5 L.-M., and Kerferd 1985). Protagoras (80B2 D.-K. = 31D7, R2 L.-M.), Lycophron (83.2 D.-K. = 38D1 L.-M.), and probably Xeniades (81.1 = 39R1 L.-M.) also polemicized against Parmenides and Zeno. Cicero states – unfortunately, in a very succinct way – that Prodicus and Thrasymachus, too, investigated the nature of things (*De natura rerum*, 84B3 D.-K. = 34D2 L.-M.; and 85A9 D.-K. = 35D4 L.-M.); and Aristophanes describes Prodicus (and the sophist Socrates) as a 'meteorosophist' (which is to say, an 'expert on celestial phenomena': 84A5 D.-K. = Dram.T22–4 L.-M.).[1] Finally, recent studies

[1] Other testimonies about Prodicus' naturalistic interests – in particular, that of Galen – have been collected by Mayhew 2011: T 61–9 (see also Mayhew 2011: 171–5, on Aristotle's testimony as a source for reconstructing Prodicus' cosmology).

have quite rightly emphasized the relationship between Antiphon and Democritus; and the former's relationship with Anaxagoras is yet to be fully investigated.[2] This succinct outline is enough to bring out an evident yet largely overlooked fact: the sophists were not interested in the thought of the natural philosophers in general (this category being so broad as to prove generic); rather, as one would expect, they focused on the more recent natural philosophers, starting from Parmenides and the Eleatic school. By and large, the investigations conducted by many sophists constitute a response to the great challenge of Parmenidean monism and an attempt to defend the multiplicity of our world – although many details are yet to be clarified. In this respect, the sophists' reflections run parallel to and intersect with those of the so-called pluralists: Empedocles, Anaxagoras, and Democritus.

In the following pages, I will endeavour to assess the importance of this engagement. But before proceeding any further, it is necessary to get back to a crucial point, namely the fact that the sophists do not constitute a homogeneous school: just as they argued with their predecessors, they heatedly argued with one another. As we will see, many of Antiphon's theses gain significance in opposition to Protagoras, and much the same probably holds true for Gorgias, Xeniades, and Lycophron. This also confirms the richness and liveliness of the debate, which gave rise to some fundamental philosophical positions that Plato and Aristotle were bound to engage with.

Protagoras' truth: the epistemological interpretation

One of Protagoras' most famous treatises was entitled *Truth*. In itself, this title is revealing of the ambitions that lay behind it: 'truth' was a key term for the Presocratics (Detienne 2006);[3] in choosing it, Protagoras clearly sought to enter into the debate by challenging a long-established tradition. The first sentence of the treatise fully confirms its author's provocative intentions: 'Of all things the measure is man: of those that are, that they are; and of those that are not, that they are

[2] Hourcade 2001. Within the same context, we may also mention those testimonies apparently concerning a 'sophistic theory of perception' (Ioli 2010: 56–9, following in the footsteps of Monique Dixsaut). Indeed, Platonic passages such as *Theaetetus*, 153e–154a, and *Meno*, 76d, may be taken to suggest that Protagoras and Gorgias had somehow adopted the Presocratic theories envisaging sense-perception in terms of the flow of particles.

[3] Detienne 2006.

not' (80B1 D.-K. = 32D9 L.-M.; for the sake of convenience, in the following pages this sentence will be abbreviated as 'man-measure').[4]

'Man-measure' is one of the few authentic Protagoras fragments to have been preserved, and many ancient sources confirm that the statement was originally formulated precisely in these terms. The problem, however, is its opacity: even in antiquity there was intense debate concerning what Protagoras really meant, and modern readings have only increased doubts about its content. As a matter of fact, it cannot be ruled out that a certain degree of ambiguity was intentional. *Truth* was not a scientific treatise but, in all likelihood, an *epideixis*, the text of a public performance. In opening his speech, Protagoras sought to capture the attention of his audience (or reader) by making a striking and allusive claim – at the expense of exactness and precision – and putting aside all caution and hesitation (which are hardly the most valuable qualities for a public performance). There is nothing strange in any of this, since a desire to capture the audience's attention was quite typical of the sophists, as is confirmed by many other sources.[5]

This is not to say that the 'man-measure' thesis had no specific meaning. Simply, it is a matter of dealing with potentially ambiguous elements. In particular, it is necessary to clarify the notion of man: that is, whether 'man' refers to each individual or to humanity in general; in discussing this issue, the meaning of the other terms that make up the sentence will also become clearer. In turn, this will help us assess the underlying meaning of Protagoras' statement and its field of applicability, so as to determine whether it is an epistemological thesis (a thesis concerning knowledge) or whether it also carries practical or political implications. By way of anticipating my argument, I note here that the sentence can be read on different levels, in line with the archaic logic according to which there is no need to clearly distinguish the different meanings possessed by a term.

There are three main sources for the 'man-measure' thesis: Plato, Aristotle, and Sextus Empiricus (a second-century CE sceptic). All

[4] The sceptic Sextus Empiricus, one of our most important sources, attributes this sentence to a work entitled *Kataballontes logoi* (*The Overthrower Arguments* or, better, *The Knockdown Arguments*; on this translation, see Appendix 2): one possible solution may be that *Truth* was one of the discourses in the *Antilogies*, which were also known with the (sub)title of *Kataballontes logoi*: see Decleva Caizzi 1999: 317. Among the most important studies, see Vlastos 1956; Decleva Caizzi 1978; Barnes 1979: ii.541–53; Mansfeld 1981; Farrar 1988.

[5] The sentence introducing the treatise on the gods was just as provocative: see Chapter 6, p. 112.

three understand the phrase – at any rate at a primary level – as though 'man' referred to 'each individual'. The most interesting testimony is in all probability that of Plato, who repeatedly engages with Protagoras' thought in his dialogues, especially the *Theaetetus* and *Protagoras*. In the *Theaetetus*, Socrates and the young mathematician Theaetetus extensively discuss the 'man-measure' thesis, regarding Protagoras as an early empiricist thinker. The Protagorean phrase is equated with the claim that 'knowledge is sensation', and paraphrased as follows: 'just as each thing appears to me, so too it is for me, and just as it appears to you, so too again for you'. Thus, if the wind appears warm to me, it is warm for me; and if it appears cold to another person, it is cold for him or her (*Theaetetus*, 152a = 80B1 D.-K. = 31R5 L.-M.). In other words, 'man-measure' means that each person is the measure of his or her own sensations, and Protagoras emerges as a staunch supporter of an empiricist epistemology that grounds knowledge in sensory data.

Plato's testimony is crucial and his reconstruction is also taken up by other authors (see 80A16 D.-K. = 31R28 L.-M. and 70B1 D.-K.). In and of itself, however, it is a reductive interpretation that risks proving misleading, as far as the meaning of 'man' is concerned. The limits of Plato's testimony become quite evident if we consider the underlying aim of the *Theaetetus*, which is not to accurately report the theses of Plato's opponent, but to show their philosophical limits. According to Plato, the 'man-measure' thesis is a muddled one; the only way to make it clear is by assuming that Protagoras was only speaking of sensations; and since (according to Plato) it is impossible to base knowledge on sensations alone, it follows that the thesis is fallacious. In other words, the discussion on Protagoras is intended to be a refutation of his thesis. The point here is not to evaluate the legitimacy of Plato's criticism (who anticipates or inaugurates one of the most important problems in the history of philosophy, namely the clash between rationalism and empiricism). What matters is the fact that a strict empiricist reading stems from a polemical interpretation, which may be philosophically legitimate but is not historically reliable: clearly, Protagoras was not speaking of sensations alone. Remarkably, Plato himself suggests that Protagoras' phrase had a broader meaning between the lines of the *Theaetetus*, in certain passages where it emerges that 'man-measure' also concerned all opinions and judgements (see 157d and 170a–171a). Aristotle and Sextus Empiricus further confirm the need for a broader interpretation: what are at play are not just sensations but more generally all opinions and judgements (and especially value judgements). 'Man is the measure of all things' means that each individual is the ultimate arbiter of all of his or her own judgements – that the wind is warm or cold, but also that performing a given action is right or wrong.[6]

The point just made is crucial in order to reconstruct the overall meaning of Protagoras' position. The transition to a broader conception of human activities (not only sense-perceptions but human judgements as a whole) brings out one aspect of the thesis that scholars have all too often overlooked. Usually it is taken for granted that Protagoras' thesis concerned problems related to human knowledge and that these problems were addressed in abstract terms, by examining the general ways in which the process of knowledge acquisition unfolds – in other words, by investigating what happens to a subject X who at a given moment *t* experiences sensation *f* (let us think of the example of the wind). Yet this is not correct. It is certainly true that Protagoras' thesis was concerned with human knowledge. However, it is not true that it focused on it in an 'abstract' way, as though humans were 'automata' that can be stimulated from the outside so as to study their reactions at given moments and in specific circumstances. This approach might work in the case of the wind, but not in that of judgements concerning what is good or bad. 'Man' refers to the individual, yet not to an abstract subject: Protagoras has concrete, historically well-defined people in mind, with their ideas and prejudices. What is meant by 'man', therefore, is each person with his or her own personal history, experiences, and expectations: that is, people for whom some options are possible while others are not, and whose judgements largely reflect their individual experience – people who are responsible for the opinions they have and for what they do. When I claim that a certain thing or action is good (or beautiful or unjust), I do so on the basis of a series of ideas and opinions that I have acquired over the course of my life and that I have continued to put to the test through my engagement with facts – in other words, on the basis of my experience, which is different from that of other people. The true measure, then, is not 'man' in the abstract sense but rather each individual's

[6] To be more precise, it must be noted that Protagoras, like many thinkers of his day, does not distinguish between the mind and sense-perceptions as though they concerned two completely different domains (i.e. the intelligible world and the sensible one): cf. 80A1 D.-K = 31R13 L.-M. on the soul.

experience.[7] The ultimate purpose of Protagoras' statement is to re-evaluate human experiences; as we shall soon see, it also carries a polemical undertone with respect to the previous tradition.

Having clarified the meaning of 'man', we can now turn to consider the second part of the phrase, 'of those that are, that they are; and of those that are not, that they are not'. Essentially, it is a matter of clarifying what 'things' means and in what sense man 'measures' them. Based on what has been noted so far, we can reasonably claim that what Protagoras meant by 'things' was not just material objects and entities (things that can be perceived by the senses, such as wind): 'things' are to be understood in their broadest possible sense as 'facts' – for example, the wind, but also an event such as performing a certain action, and all that happens to man. In this respect, the term chosen by Protagoras is highly revealing. *Chrema* derives from the verb *chraomai*, meaning 'to treat', 'to use', 'to entertain a relation with': according to its original meaning, the term describes not so much 'things' in themselves (for in this case Protagoras could have used *onta* or *pragmata*), as in their relation to us; the emphasis is on the way in which we relate to things, use them, judge them, and so on. 'Things', then, means everything which human beings enter into contact with: material objects but also events and occurrences – in other words, facts.

As far as the notion of measure is concerned, it is clear that man is the measure not of the existence of things (such as the wind or the occurrence of a certain action), but rather of the way in which things present themselves (for example, as warm/cold or good/bad). The expression, that is, must be understood not in an existential sense (in which case it would be difficult to understand what it means for man to be the measure of the non-existence of the things that are not), but rather in a modal-predicative sense. Protagoras is not denying the existence of the external world, but only limiting the possibility of knowing it to the way in which it presents itself to our experience (hence, if I judge the wind to be warm, I am the measure of the fact that it is warm and not of the fact that it exists; if I judge the wind not to be warm, I am measure of the fact that it is not warm and not of the fact that it does not exist). Things in themselves do not possess any predetermined truth or any intrinsic value: they simply exist, they

[7] Mansfeld 1981: 44–6.

are what surrounds a person, what happens to him or her. What matters is the way in which we relate to them: each individual, according to his or her experience, is the judge of these facts, insofar as he or she assigns them a degree of consistency or value.

This initial reconstruction also enables us to evaluate Protagoras' position with respect to the previous intellectual tradition: 'man-measure' emerges as a polemical response to the enquiries on *physis* conducted by many Presocratics, and in particular to Parmenides' monism.[8] Protagoras' interest in critically engaging with the Eleatic school is confirmed by other sources: in particular, Porphyry (a third–fourth-century CE Neoplatonist) informs us that Protagoras wrote a treatise *On Being* (regrettably lost) against those who 'uphold the uniqueness of being' – clearly, Parmenides and his disciples (80B2 D.-K. = 31D7, R2 L.-M.); a polemic with Zeno is also attested.[9] The same polemical intentions are suggested by Plato's *Theaetetus*, which presents Protagoras and Parmenides as the leading exponents of two opposite ways of conceiving reality, namely as becoming and as being.

Once again, although Plato's testimony is crucial, it must be examined with great caution, so as to avoid pushing our interpretation of Protagoras too far. The *Theaetetus* ascribes a sort of radical Heracliteanism to Protagoras that presents reality as the constant flow of all things, a flow so incessant that we should speak not of 'being'

[8] Farrar 1988: 48–50.

[9] See 29A29 D.-K. = Zen. D12b L.-M.: 'For he [Zeno] said: "Tell me, Protagoras, does one grain of millet make a sound when it falls or does the thousandth part of the grain of millet?" When the other answered that it did not, he said, "Does a medimnus of grains of millet make a sound or not when it falls?" When the other answered that it did make a noise, Zeno said, "Well then, is there not a proportion between a medimnus of grains of millet and a single grain and the thousandth part of that one grain?" And when the other answered that there was one, Zeno said, "Well then, will there not be the same proportions between the sounds with regard to one another? For just as the things are that make a sound, so too are their sounds; and since that is so, if a medimnus of millet makes a sound, a single grain of millet will make a sound too, and so too the thousandth part of that grain"'. While not impossible in chronological terms, it seems unlikely that the meeting between the two thinkers really occurred. However, this passage may still be seen to provide further evidence of the polemical exchanges that the sophist entertained with the Eleatic school. The text in question has sometimes been interpreted as proof of the fact that Protagoras denied infinite divisibility; but this seems like an incorrect conclusion, since Protagoras – at least in theory – does not deny the possibility of a division into increasingly small parts. What he denies is rather that the sound produced by these portions of millet is audible. Once again, we may note that the sophist examined things from the point of view of sensible experience, against the abstractions of the natural philosophers: just as sight does not perceive the touching of a sphere and a tangent at a given point (see 80B7 D.-K. =31D33 L.-M.), so hearing can only perceive sounds up to a certain point. Even from this perspective, man is the *measure* of all things.

but only of 'becoming'. On the opposite side of the spectrum, according to the dialogue, stands Parmenides, the philosopher of the stability of being. This thesis, however, is conditioned by the empiricist interpretation, whose limits I have already highlighted: if we only speak of sensations, it is clear that what we have in mind is a world exclusively made up of material objects (since sensations are only engendered starting from material things, such as a table or the wind); and if sensations vary (in the sense that the wind will appear warm at one time and cold at another), this occurs because material reality varies, changing constantly. In other words, the notion that Protagoras supported a fluxist interpretation of reality rests on the assumption that he was referring to sensations alone. But this, as we have seen, is a reductive interpretation. Significantly, Plato referred to this thesis as Protagoras' 'secret doctrine' (*Theaetetus*, 152c), thereby revealing that it was not a thesis openly upheld by the sophist, but rather a position that in his view could legitimately be inferred from his claims.[10]

Protagoras' engagement with Parmenides does not actually take place on the ontological level. His main interest was not to oppose a different (and truer) world to that of Parmenides (the world of becoming to the world of being, as Plato would have it) – a cosmology capable of accounting for the multiplicity of natural entities.[11] In this respect, Protagoras differs from the so-called 'pluralist' philosophers Empedocles, Anaxagoras, and Democritus, who, in response to Parmenides, had sought to 'save the phenomena'. Protagoras rather set out to 'save man': his challenge was a more radical one, and it targeted the very assumptions on which Parmenides' reflection rested. For Parmenides (like many other natural philosophers), terms such as 'man' and 'opinion' were synonymous with error, by contrast to the truth and being: in his view, the purpose of philosophy was to investigate the universal and absolute first principles. Even the multifaceted

[10] On this passage, see Zilioli 2013: 239–43, arguing that Plato's text attributes to Protagoras not so much a radical version of a Heraclitean theory of flux as a theory of ontological indeterminacy; and Corradi 2012: 79–89.

[11] This does not rule out the possibility that Protagoras' conception of material reality may have been similar to that of other Presocratics, but it is important to stress once again that this was not the sophist's chief interest. In brief, and without delving into the details, it cannot be ruled out that Protagoras viewed physical reality as something that contains all opposites. If this is the case, the sophist was only taking up a thesis that was common among natural philosophers and typical of the polarizing thought of the Presocratics, who were used to envisaging nature in terms of contrasting or harmonizing opposites (let us think here of the Pythagoreans or of Heraclitus). This is Sextus Empiricus' interpretation (*Outlines of Pyrrhonism*, 1.216–19 = 80A14 D.-K. = 31R21 L.-M.), cf. Woodruff 1999: 303–4.

world of humankind was to be investigated with the same perspective, by identifying its points of contact with being and subordinating what is relative or contingent within it. In other words, Parmenides (a) had drawn a clear line between the true world of being on the one hand and the world of appearances and becoming on the other, while (b) asserting the possibility of a privileged form of knowledge that moves beyond the illusory world surrounding us in order to reach true reality (the truth of being), and (c) discrediting ordinary human knowledge (unfounded opinions).

Protagoras opposed all these assumptions: (b) because nobody enjoys privileged access to these alleged higher 'realities'; (a) because no-one can ignore the reality that surrounds us, and which is our one and only world; and (c) because it is not true that the world that surrounds us is helplessly muddled and corrupt, since through our judgements we are capable of 'measuring' it and giving it an order – which is to say, of knowing it. There are no wise men and ignorant people, then: each man can legitimately express his own opinions and judgements. Protagoras reverses Parmenides' perspective, reappraising the uniqueness of human experience, which is always relative and contingent: this relativeness and contingency is not a limit but rather the condition on the basis of which we relate to things. Instead of developing hypotheses on the nature of the all, we should shift our focus back to our everyday life in order to solve the problems affecting it. This was the programmatic (and polemical) message conveyed by the first sentence of the treatise on *Truth*, as discussed by Versenyi:

> The things we are concerned with are *chremata*, i.e. things we are decisively related to; thus there is no point in speaking in a grand manner about what things may or may not be in themselves; what we have to take into account and concentrate on is what they are for us, in the world we live in, in a world in which our relationship to things, our living in the world, is decisive.[12]

Protagoras' position has been described in many different ways. Much emphasis has been placed on his 'subjectivism', stressing the importance of the subject for the sophist; yet interpreters have also spoken of 'objectivism', noting once again that the 'man-measure' thesis presupposes a real and concrete relation with reality.[13] Other scholars have spoken of phenomenalism, stressing the fact that reality always

[12] Versenyi 1962: 181.

[13] More recently, see also the 'pluralist' reading developed by Apfel 2011: 45–78.

presents itself as a phenomenon, as that which appears. Like all '-isms', these classifications are valid as long as we remember that they are merely tools that may help identify the important aspects of Protagoras' thesis, and not formulas that miraculously explain everything. Given this caveat, the category that probably best describes the particularity and originality of Protagoras' thought is that of relativism.[14] Knowledge always depends on the existing circumstances and the knowing subjects, which is why it makes no sense to speak of a single and absolute truth: truth is the relationship which each person establishes with surrounding reality. There is no one absolute truth, only as many truths as there are perceiving and judging subjects.

Protagoras' truth: the practical and political consequences

The thesis that man is the measure of his own judgements faces two serious objections: the charge that it is self-refuting and the charge of solipsism. Protagoras was at least partly aware of these two difficulties, and clarifying them will help us bring out the richness and significance of his thesis.

The charge of being self-refuting (or *peritrope*, as the ancients called it: literally, the charge of 'tripping up') was apparently formulated for the first time by Democritus (80A15 D.-K. = 68A114 D.-K. = 31R22 L.-M.) and then further developed by Plato (in the *Theaetetus* and *Euthydemus*) and Aristotle (in the fourth book of the *Metaphysics*). In brief, this accusation states that, if all judgements are true (this being the implicit meaning of the 'man-measure' thesis), then the judgement that 'man-measure' is false is also true; hence, 'man-measure' is false. Protagoras had further claimed that 'it is not possible to contradict' (80A19 D.-K. = 31R10 L.-M.) and this led Plato and Aristotle to add that the sophist denied the principle of non-contradiction, suggesting another version of the *peritrope* charge: Protagoras claims that all judgements are true (let us call this thesis P) and his opponent that Protagoras' claim is false (non-P); but, according to Protagoras, contradiction is impossible and therefore non-P is compatible with P. But in this case, non-P is true; hence, P is false.[15]

[14] See Woodruff 1999: 300–4; Lee 2005: 30–45; Zilioli 2013. On the adoption of this category with reference to Protagoras and the sophists, consider the cautious note sounded by Bett 1989.

[15] Barnes 1979: ii.548.

The soundness of this criticism has been the object of a heated scholarly debate, yet no shared solution has been reached.[16] Protagoras could nonetheless resort to a few arguments to defend his views. The accusation omits the qualifiers 'for me' and 'for you', which are crucial to the 'man-measure' thesis. By introducing these qualifiers, Protagoras could reformulate the *peritrope* charge in such a way as to neutralize it: if what I judge is true and I judge that Protagoras' thesis is false, it does not follow from this that Protagoras' thesis is false in an absolute sense, but only that it is false 'for me'. And the fact that it is false 'for me' does not prevent it from being true for other people: it remains true, for instance, for Protagoras, who can thus avoid the charge that he is tripping himself up (as well as denying the principle of non-contradiction).

This defensive strategy, however, is potentially open to an even more serious charge, that of solipsism. This risk is clearly present in the aforementioned thesis that it is 'impossible to contradict'. The thesis in question is fully compatible with 'man-measure', for if each individual is the measure of his or her own world of sensations and judgements, contradiction can only be apparent: each individual entertains a relationship with things whose truth-reality cannot be contradicted or disputed by others. Still, it is just as evident that people differ, since some maintain what others deny. But how can we deal with these divergences and oppositions, if everyone is right? If this is how things stand, what follows is a radical (and intolerable) form or solipsism, whereby the fact that each person is his or her own judge makes it impossible to decide things with others. The price that Protagoras must pay in order to defend the consistency of his doctrines seems far too high.[17]

In this case, too, Protagoras has a number of good arguments on his side. Up until this point, the discussion has centred on the problem of 'truth', a concept the importance of which can hardly be disputed. However, no matter how central it may be, truth is not the only criterion that governs human thoughts and actions. Alongside truth there are other, equally important criteria. One is 'what is useful': all judgements are true, but some are more expedient than others. And this is what matters the most for Protagoras. To exploit a compelling formula, Marcel Detienne described the Presocratic thinkers as 'masters of

[16] Burnyeat 1976; Lee 2005: 46–76; and especially Castagnoli 2010.
[17] Woodruff 1999: 303.

truth'; Protagoras (along with all sophists) might instead be called the 'master of usefulness'.

Once more, with regard to what is useful, the most important testimony comes from Plato.[18] As we have seen, the main object of the *Theaetetus* is knowledge, and it is in relation to this problem that Plato introduces, discusses, and criticizes Protagoras' thesis. However, the dialogue also features a lengthy digression that, while it does not directly touch upon epistemological problems, nonetheless helps to clarify Protagoras' perspective in all of its complexity: this is the so-called 'Apology of Protagoras' (166a–168c), a lengthy speech that Protagoras would have delivered, had he had the opportunity to take part in the dialogue (the dialogue of the *Theaetetus* takes place in 399 BC, the year of Socrates' trial, by which time Protagoras had already died). In his fictional reply, Protagoras accuses Socrates of playing the sophist and of intentionally deceiving his interlocutors by playing on the affinity between the words 'to know'/'to have knowledge' and 'to be wise'/'to have wisdom'. But, the sophist continues, the truth-value of a type of wisdom is one thing, the value of its contents another: if we are to reason correctly, we must not confuse these two things. Unlike the former, which is changeless, the latter varies: from the point of view of knowledge and truth, every individual is a measure, and the fact that each person is a measure depends on his or her relationship with the things that surrounds him or her – this is a fact. But from the point of view of the value of the contents (of wisdom), it cannot be ruled out that some people are capable of showing the individual how to establish a more expedient relationship with reality.

Socrates puts the following words into Protagoras' mouth:

> For I myself say that the truth is just as I wrote it: each of us is the measure of the things that are and of those that are not, but one person differs enormously from another precisely inasmuch as things exist and appear to be something for one person, something else for another. As for wisdom (*sophia*) and the wise man (*sophos*), I am very far from saying that they do not exist; but I also call the man wise who, by transforming things, makes them appear to be good and be good for someone to whom they appeared to be bad and were bad.
>
> (*Theaetetus*, 166d = 80A21 D.-K. = 31D38 L.-M.; transl. after L.-M.)

[18] Very interesting considerations regarding the problem of what is useful and its relativity may be found in Guthrie 1971: 164–75. De facto, the relativity of what is useful may be understood both in an objective sense (the usefulness of a thing varies depending on the people or circumstances) and in a subjective sense (nothing is good or bad in itself: it is we who establish this). The first sense best expresses Protagoras' position.

Thus, to a sick person food will appear bad and be bad: it would be meaningless to argue that the sick person is wrong to say that food tastes bitter to him or her. However, there is someone, namely the doctor, who can help the sick person build a more expedient relationship with reality, by ensuring that food will taste sweet, not bitter, to them. Protagoras' aim is not merely to abolish the idea of truth, which is shattered into an endless number of private truths; his aim is to replace this criterion with another, more effective criterion – that of what is useful. It is by reflecting on the issue of what is useful that the sophist, while respecting everybody's opinion, shows his wisdom. For, ultimately, what is useful varies from one situation to the next (80A22 D.-K.), and the sophist's task is to identify what is truly expedient in each case. Therefore, just as the doctor helps the patient's body, so the sophist can help his patient build a better, more expedient relationship with reality: relying on his experience, the sophist can help his pupil evaluate his or her beliefs and whether he or she regards them as being truly important, or whether they are merely values that he or she has passively inherited from tradition. The sophist can verify whether the pupil's system of values is consistent, or whether it includes contrasting beliefs. Finally, the sophist can give the pupil advice on how to set out to achieve his or her goals. In brief, we may conclude that Protagoras teaches only one, fundamental thing: how to judge well on the basis of the existing circumstances.[19]

By focusing on the criterion of what is useful, Protagoras can thus justify his teaching within a context in which the space for truth has been substantially limited: the wisdom he claims to possess does not stem from any privileged access to an imaginary higher realm of ultimate truths from which other people are barred. Rather, his wisdom is based on his experience and his capacity to master arguments and problems: it is a human form of knowledge that is never conclusive but nonetheless has its usefulness, insofar as it can help the pupil understand what is best for him or her and how to achieve it. Protagoras' teaching takes the form not of a transmission of data and information, but of a means to establish a more effective relationship with reality.

The significance of Protagoras' wisdom emerges even more clearly in relation to political problems, the field in which he most flaunted his competences. In a famous passage from another Platonic dialogue,

[19] Woodruff 1999: 309; Woodruff 2013.

the *Protagoras*, the sophist claims that what he teaches is essentially how to make the best decisions with respect not only to private matters but also (and especially) to the affairs of the city, noting immediately afterwards that this is the 'political art' (*politike techne*).[20] The object of politics is the contrast between the potentially conflictual values of different people: everyone has his or her own ideas, values, and aims. However, these values and aims often differ or even clash, and this creates the premises for conflict. Here is where the opportunity arises for the sophist to intervene. Like everyone else, Protagoras cannot claim to objectively know what is good or expedient in absolute terms. But, unlike many other people, he possesses certain practical competences and knows how to foster a critical reflection among citizens to help them reach an agreement on what is best for everyone – to help them identify those values (which are not absolute values, but ones that can always be reappraised) that make it possible to establish a better relation among the individuals of the community, as well as with reality. The sophist can do so not only in those rare cases in which he can directly participate in the political life of a city, but also indirectly, by teaching his pupils to become good politicians, which is to say politicians capable of building a consensus that will defuse the risk of conflict. In both cases, Protagoras' wisdom proves crucial for the life of the *polis*, and in particular for that of a democratic *polis* such as Athens.[21] Protagoras' wisdom is not divine but human and, most importantly, political.

To conclude, we can reappraise the overall meaning of the 'man-measure' thesis. The introduction of the criterion of what is useful entails a significant shift of perspective. The thesis undoubtedly concerns the problem of knowledge, but it is important to stress that it is not limited to epistemological issues; rather, one might argue that Protagoras is chiefly concerned with the problem of knowledge in relation to its practical consequences. The problem of truth is not just an epistemological problem, but also a practical one. Consequently, the term 'man' acquires a different meaning as well. The object of 'man-measure' is not just individuals but humans in their mutual relations.

[20] 'The object of my instruction is good deliberation about household matters, to know how to manage one's own household in the best way possible, and about those of the city, so as to be most capable of acting and speaking in the city's interests' (*Protagoras*, 318e–319a). Reference to the political craft is made immediately afterwards, at 319a (both passages are included in the Diels-Kranz edition as testimony 80A5 = 31D37 L.-M.).

[21] Guthrie 1971: 174–5.

Protagoras' statement therefore implies increasing degrees of complexity, leading from the individual to the *polis* (understood as a human community): if I am the measure of my own judgements, then we as members of our community are judges of our own decisions. In this sense, it is possible to note that 'man' stands not just for every individual but for human beings in general, who in the absence of absolute truths jointly establish those values which will enable them to live together in the best possible way.

A detailed analysis of the available sources thus reveals the significance and richness of the 'man-measure' thesis, which fully confirms the programmatic value that Protagoras sought to assign to it by employing it as the opening sentence of *Truth*. The statement has different, mutually compatible, interpretative levels, which reveal the complexity of the human dimension. The 'man-measure' thesis tackles the problem of human knowledge – of what humans can know and how; in this respect, it upholds the importance of each individual's experiences, in open opposition to the previous philosophical tradition. The thesis, however, also concerns practical matters: not just what we can know and how, but how we can act. As we will see later on, political reflection arguably constitutes the most interesting aspect of Protagoras' speculation. What is important to note at this stage is that the political aspects of his thought, of which he was so proud, closely depend on his ontological and epistemological theses, in the light of which he defines the human experience.

Gorgias: the dialectic of not-being

Even more provocative than Protagoras' *Truth* was Gorgias' text *On Not-Being or on Nature* (82B3 D.-K. = 32D26 L.-M.). 'Nature' was a key term for Presocratic thinkers, who used it to describe reality as a whole. Nature, in other words, coincides with total reality, with that which is: with being, as the Parmenidean Melissus had concluded by entitling his treatise *On Nature or On Being*. If, as would seem to be the case,[22] the title was indeed chosen by Gorgias himself, what we

[22] The question of titles is always a thorny one for archaic and classical authors. However, as rightly noted by Palmer 2009: 205 n. 25, the peculiarity of Melissus' and Gorgias' titles would seem to suggest that they are authentic and that the latter was probably drawing upon the former. On the possible dating of the text to the mid-fifth century BC (or, more precisely, to the years 444–

have is a paradoxical equating of reality with nothingness.[23] Gorgias' treatise represents the complete 'overturning' of the Presocratics' grand investigation of nature, or rather its negation: in typical fashion, the sophist's argument rests on an intellectual tradition in order to overthrow it.[24]

Regrettably, the original text is lost – and with it, in all likelihood, many of the subtleties of Gorgias' style and arguments. Still, the sources at our disposal give us a good enough idea of the content of this treatise and of the genuine *tour de force* that Gorgias imposed on his public.[25] As far as we can tell, the text consisted of a tight sequence of arguments in defence of three paradoxical theses: 'Gorgias says that nothing is; and if [*sc.* something] is, it is unknowable; and if [*sc.* something] both is and is knowable, it cannot be indicated to other people' (*M.X.G.* 979a12–13 = D26 L.-M.). What were Gorgias' more general aims? In order to answer this question, we need to examine the arguments used in support of each of the three theses. In favour of the first thesis, according to which nothing exists, Gorgias put forward two series of arguments, by developing some personal arguments and by dialectically exploiting his opponents' theses (the anonymous author of *M.X.G.* explicitly mentions Melissus and Zeno: 979a22–3). In 'Gorgias' own argument', the chief topic of discussion is the crucial contrast between being and not-being (979a25–33); in the dialectical demonstration, what Gorgias investigated was instead some of the fundamental properties of being, such as the fact of being generated or ungenerated, one or many (979b20–980a8).

The aim of the first argument is to demonstrate that neither being nor not-being can exist, which leads to the conclusion that nothing

441 BC, the date of the eighty-fourth Olympic Games: 82B2 D.-K. = 32P4 L.-M.), see the cautious remarks by Mansfeld 1985: 247 and Ioli 2010: 15–18.

23 Wardy 1996: 15.

24 Cassin 1995: 27.

25 We have two main sources: an anonymous treatise devoted to a critical discussion of the thought of Melissus, Xenophanes, and Gorgias (*On Melissus, Xenophanes, and Gorgias*, usually abbreviated to *M.X.G.*; on the identity of this author, see Ioli 2010: 23–8); and Sextus Empiricus, *Against the Mathematicians*, 7.65–87. Despite the evident similarities, these two texts arrange Gorgias' writing in different ways: the more reliable source is probably *M.X.G.* (which I will be following); Sextus' discussion (the only one published in the Diels-Kranz edition) appears instead to reflect a desire to reshape Gorgias' arguments by lending them a sceptical twist. Particularly crucial are the analyses provided by Calogero 1932; Newiger 1973; and Mansfeld 1985. Among other modern editions, I shall refer to Cassin 1980; Buchheim 1989; and Ioli 2010 and 2013.

is.[26] In order to reach this goal, Gorgias develops his argument in two stages: first he establishes the identity between being and not-being, demonstrating that even not-being is; from this he derives two consequences that lead to the impossibility of both being and not-being, and hence to the conclusion that nothing is. The argumentative structure is always the same: (a) first Gorgias establishes a starting assumption; (b) then he explicates what follows from it; (c) he explains the reasons for this consequence; and finally (d) he draws his conclusions. Here is a schematic reconstruction of the whole passage:

I. Identify being with not-being
   (a) starting assumption: if not-being *is* not-being;
   (b) consequence: what is not *is* no less than what is *is*;
   (c) explanation: for what is not *is* what it is not, and what is *is* what it is;
   (d) conclusion: hence, not-being *is* as much as being.[27]

This conclusion raises two distinct problems (not-being *is*; not-being *is* in a similar way to being), which are analysed as follows:

II.1. First consequence
   (a) starting assumption: if not-being *is*;
   (b) consequence: being, its opposite, *is* not;
   (c) explanation: for if not-being *is*, then being, its opposite, *is* not;
   (d) conclusion: hence, nothing is.

II.2. Second consequence
   (a) starting assumption: if being and not-being are the same thing;
   (b) consequence: being *is* not;
   (c) explanation: for what *is* not *is not-being*, and hence even what is *is not-being*;
   (d) conclusion: hence, nothing *is*.

As has rightly been observed, 'G[orgias]' own argument' presents 'a novel exploration' of the notion of being and not-being, thanks to its polemical reworking of Parmenides' theses.[28] Indeed, the meaning of the first thesis becomes clearer if we view it in relation to a fundamental

[26] The most convincing analyses are found in Calogero 1932: 189–268; Mansfeld 1985; Striker 1996: 11–14; Palmer 1999: 66–74; Curd 2006; and Ioli 2010: 28–40.

[27] The text of the anonymous *M.X.G.* literally states: 'so that things (*pragmata*) are not more (*ouden mallon*) than they are not'. However, we should not rule out the possibility that the choice of the expression *ouden mallon* and the use of *pragma* may depend on the vocabulary (and Pyrrhonian inclinations) of the source rather than on Gorgias himself: see Mansfeld 1988: 258, followed by Curd 2006: 187 n. 8; *contra*, see Ioli 2010: 34–36.

[28] Curd 2006: 186.

verse from Parmenides' poem.[29] In presenting the two paths – that of being, which alone can be travelled, and that of not-being, which cannot even be spoken or thought of – Parmenides had written with regard to the latter 'that it is not and that it is necessary for it not to be' (28B2, 5 D.-K. = Parm. D6 L.-M.; my translation). What is the subject of this sentence? Scholars have long debated this issue; on his part, Gorgias seems to understand the 'is not' of the first hemistich as the subject of the second part of the verse, as though the meaning of the sentence were: it *is* not and it is necessary for what is not not to be. Gorgias thus exploits the ambiguity of Parmenides' use of the verb being in support of his own paradoxical thesis: his reasoning rests on the observation of the fact that if we claim that what is not *is not*, then we are de facto implying that what is not *is* something, namely what is not – just as what is *is* something, namely what is.[30] To be more precise, the ambiguity lies in the double meaning which Parmenides apparently attributes to the verb 'to be': an existential and a predicative meaning. The verb 'to be' is existential insofar as to claim that being *is* is tantamount to claiming that being exists; and it is predicative insofar as to claim that being *is* indicates the essential property which distinguishes it – a property that Parmenides clarifies further on in his poem, when he explains that the fact of being implies the fact of being ungenerated, imperishable, and so forth (if what is truly is, then it must be ungenerated, since if it were generated, it would previously have been other than what is and hence not-being, and so on: see 28B8 D.-K. = Parm. D8 L.-M.).

Gorgias' innovation lies in the fact of having applied this reasoning no longer to being but to not-being: if the essential property of what is *is to be*, the essential property of what is not *is not to be*; with regard to what is not, it must be possible to legitimately claim that somehow it *is*, namely that it *is* that which distinguishes not-being (predicative sense), and hence that it somehow *exists* (existential sense). Gorgias, in other words, brings out the tension created by the equivalence (or lack of distinction) between the predicative and existential meanings of the verb 'to be'. This lack of distinction also explains the two following passages: whereas in the first consequence the focus is on the

[29] Palmer 1999: 72.

[30] See Striker 1996: 12. This reasoning is also referred to by Plato in the *Parmenides* (162a–b: see Mansfeld 1985: 258–62; Palmer 1999: 109–17) and Aristotle in the *Metaphysics* (see 1003b10: 'It is for this reason that we say even of non-being that it *is* non-being').

existential meaning (if not-being *is*, being, its opposite, *is not*), in the second one the focus is on the predicative meaning (being *is not-being*: if being is identical to not-being, then being too *is not-being*, and hence is not). Certainly, this undue transition from one meaning of the verb 'to be' to the other risks to invalidate the formal correctness of Gorgias' refutation. But Gorgias might have objected to this that what he was doing was merely reproducing an ambiguity already to be found in Parmenides, simply applying it to not-being rather than being.[31] In this respect at least, insofar as he successfully combined being and not-being, Gorgias could have effectively defended his thesis that nothing is: for Parmenides himself had observed that the equating of being and not-being 'simply reduces both to the negative level of non-existence'.[32]

In the 'dialectical argument', Gorgias targets the speculative activities of all the Presocratics, and not just the theses of the Eleatics. Yet in this case, too, the Eleatics are Gorgias' privileged point of reference, as may be inferred from the discussion on the generated or ungenerated character of being, which probably represents the most successful example of Gorgias' way of arguing.[33] Gorgias accepts the arguments put forward by the Eleatic school regarding the impossibility for being to be generated, and adopts the thesis that being could neither be generated from what is (for, in changing, what is would no longer be what is), nor from what is not (for nothing can be generated from what is not: *nihil ex nihilo*). Hence, being is not generated. The problem, however, is that being is not ungenerated either, contrary to what the Eleatics liked to claim: Gorgias refutes the Eleatics on the basis of their very own theses, by leading the arguments that Melissus and Zeno had produced into contradiction. According to Melissus, if being were ungenerated, it would also have to be infinite. This leap from the temporal level to the spatial one might seem

[31] Calogero 1932: 197.

[32] Ioli 2010: 31; cf. 28B6, 8–9 D.-K. = Parm. D8, 8–9 L.-M. Another objection to Gorgias' reasoning is put forth by the anonymous author of *M.X.G.*, who observes that Gorgias' thesis also implies the opposite conclusion: given that being and not-being coincide, one might conclude not that nothing is, but that everything is. Yet, once again, the anti-Parmenidean polemical backdrop is enough to show that this is not a real objection at all for Gorgias, given that his primary aim is to conflate being and not-being: for Parmenides, claiming that everything is – both what is and what is not – is no more acceptable than the thesis that nothing is.

[33] On Gorgias' argumentative strategy, which often arranges his opponents' theses into contrasting pairs or multiple sets of arguments (e.g. *Encomium of Helen*, 13), see Mansfeld 1985 and 1986 and the observations made in Chapter 3, pp. 57–62.

questionable to a modern reader, but it was explicitly upheld by Melissus (30B2 D.-K. = Mel. D3 L.-M.) on the basis of the assumption that generating something means giving it form, determining it; conversely, being ungenerated means being formless, indeterminate – and hence infinite. Once this has been granted, it is easy for Gorgias to refute the Eleatics' thesis by invoking Parmenides' other great pupil: Zeno (29A24 D.-K. = Zen. D13a L.-M.) allows us to argue that if being were infinite it would be nowhere, since to be somewhere is to be contained by something and this is impossible for what is infinite. Hence, if being were ungenerated, it would be nowhere and therefore would not be at all. But if being is neither generated (as many Presocratics liked to think) nor ungenerated (as the Eleatics argued), then it is not: nothing *is*.[34]

The flow of Gorgias' texts always produces a baffling effect on the reader/listener. After having demonstrated that nothing is/exists, Gorgias admits that something might be/exist after all: but, even if it did, it still would not be knowable. This is the aim of the second thesis. Regrettably, the text of the anonymous *M.X.G.* is very corrupt here and it is almost impossible to come up with a definitive reconstruction. One plausible solution features the intertwining of two arguments.[35] The first is a paradoxical argument, which sets out once again from a Parmenidean premise, namely the close identity between being and thought (28B3, B8, 38 DK = Parm. D6, D8, 38 LM): if someone thinks of something (if he or she has something in mind), that thing is; but this means that if someone thinks of a chariot flying across the sea, then there is a chariot flying across the sea. As this is patently absurd, the conclusion is that external reality does not always coincide with what we have in mind:[36] the problem is precisely to distinguish between

[34] Briefly put, Gorgias' argument would run as follows: if *P*, then *X* or *Y*; but neither *X* nor *Y*; hence, not *P* either. A similar argumentative structure also underpins the second discussion, focusing on the issue of whether being is one or many: if being were one, it would be bodiless; but what is bodiless has no magnitude, and with no magnitude it would be nothing, as Zeno observed. On the other hand, if there is no unity, there cannot be any multiplicity either, since this depends on unity. Therefore, if being is neither one nor many, it *is not*: nothing *is*. In *M.X.G.* we then find a discussion on movement, but the fragmentary state of the text does not allow us to determine whether it constituted a further development of the reflection on unity/multiplicity or whether it instead marked the beginning of the discussion on the motion/rest pair. In support of the first (and more reasonable) hypothesis, see Ioli 2010: 46–8.

[35] Caston 2002.

[36] This point might also be raised against Protagoras, who had upheld a sort of infallibilism by denying the possibility of error: see Di Benedetto 1955 (according to whom Protagoras is actually the chief polemical target of the whole treatise); Mansfeld 1985: 249–58; Caston 2002: 217–18; Ioli 2010: 50–60.

what is true and what is false, which is to say to choose one mental state over another. This marks the beginning of the second argument, which introduces sense-perceptions by assimilating them to judgements (the introduction of sense-perceptions once again shows that Gorgias did not have the Eleatics alone in mind; rather, this second part of the reasoning seems to run against ordinary assumptions about knowledge). For, ultimately, sense-perceptions also concern thoughts: if I see a thing, that thing is in my mind. But, as has just been noted, if a thing is in my mind, that thing *is*, which leads to absurd results; hence, not even sense-perceptions are always reliable. However, if neither judgements nor sense-perceptions correctly represent reality, we are no longer capable of grasping the truth – we no longer have any way of understanding which of the things we think truly exist. The truth might exist and it might even be thinkable, but we will never know whether we have thought it. And this is tantamount to saying that, even if being *is*, it is unknowable.

In the transition from the second to the third thesis, Gorgias concedes what he had first denied: after having established that being is unknowable, he allows that it might be knowable; but even if it might be knowable, it cannot be communicated to other people. Besides, we may grant that reality exists, and that we know reality, but we cannot grant that we can communicate our knowledge. This, as we shall see, is the most important point for Gorgias, a point that is never disputed in the treatise. He appears to adduce three arguments in defence of the third thesis (in this case, too, the text is corrupt – the most convincing analysis remains that of Mourelatos 1985). The first argument rests on the assumption of the heterogeneity of *logos* (understood as thought and discourse) with respect to reality. Just as sight does not see sound, and hearing does not hear colours, so *logos* does not speak things, but words: the only possible experience is direct, first-hand experience. But this is off-limits for *logos*, which always represents a translation of such experience, a failed translation insofar as it proves incapable of taking the place of its object.[37] The other two arguments merely reassert the isolation of *logos*, showing that there is no way of confirming whether what A has communicated has been received by B as A

[37] An alternative reconstruction that is worth mentioning is the one suggested by Wardy 1996: 14–21, who justifies the impossibility of transmitting *logos* on the basis of a physicalist interpretation of it: *logoi* are not symbols but physical objects; as such, they can only occur in one place at any one moment; clearly, this makes the transmission of *the same logos* impossible.

understands it; indeed, not even A can be sure of this, given the divergence between his own perceptions and feelings at different times. An unbridgeable gulf thus separates things from thoughts and words: even assuming that being is knowable, it cannot be communicated.[38]

Now that we have reached the end of this analysis, it is time to evaluate Gorgias' treatise in all of its complexity. What are the aims of this treatise and what is its underlying meaning? Certainly, the treatise contains a fair dose of irony and provocation, both in the theses it defends and in the way in which it defends them. The problem, then, is to understand the meaning of these provocations. Scholars in the past fluctuated between two radical interpretations of Gorgias: the first dismissed his text as a mere *divertissement* of no real philosophical interest;[39] the second interpretation emphasized its 'nihilism'.[40] It is all too evident, however, that both theses are one-sided, and that they fail to adequately account for the challenge launched by Gorgias. A certain playfulness, which frequently manifests itself in the author's desire to dazzle his public with bold arguments, no doubt constitutes a defining feature of Gorgias' practice (and of the sophists' more in general).[41] Yet this does not justify the conclusion that there is nothing of philosophical relevance in the treatise (and that the treatise is merely an example of sophistry – of arguments that are only apparently true[42]). On the contrary, we only need to think of the discussions on the verb 'to be' or of the problem of communicability to realize that Gorgias is raising questions of the utmost importance, which all great philosophers – from Plato to those of our own day – have felt compelled to address.[43] As for the 'nihilist' reading, even leaving aside the problem of what 'nihilist' means, it is clear that this is a doubly selective interpretation. First, it de facto only considers the first thesis – that nothing

[38] Kerferd 1984: 218–21; Palmer 2009: 87–8.

[39] See Gomperz 1912: 28.

[40] One notable example of this interpretation is furnished by Diels 1884, which reconstructs Gorgias' spiritual history in three stages: after initially subscribing to Empedocles' theses, Gorgias discovered Eleatic dialectic, which marked the beginning of a 'period of doubt, or rather of despair', culminating with the nihilism of the treatise on not-being; Gorgias then emerged from this nihilism through a new interest in rhetoric. The nihilistic interpretation crops up again and again in the literature (see the list in Caston 2002: 205 n. 1) and has recently been taken up again by Hourcade 2006.

[41] Consider too fragment 82B12 D.-K. = 32D18 L.-M.: 'Gorgias said that we should destroy our opponents' seriousness by laughter, and their laughter by seriousness.'

[42] See J. Robinson 1973.

[43] Besides, as rightly noted by Kerferd 1955–6: 3, Gorgias' treatise is just as playful as Plato's *Parmenides* (see *Parm.* 137b).

is – while the problem which Gorgias is most concerned with is the third, namely that which concerns the split between language and reality. Secondly, even if we were only to take into consideration the first part, Gorgias' polemical target are the views of the Eleatics and the other Presocratic thinkers: what Gorgias would be denying are metaphysical entities such as Parmenides' being or the atoms of Leucippus and Democritus. But this hardly justifies the thesis that Gorgias was a 'nihilist' (at most, one could argue that the supporters of the theses criticized by Gorgias – Parmenides and the other Presocratics – were nihilists).

What are more interesting, albeit not fully satisfactory, are two other interpretations which have been put forward. The first one, the 'subjectivist' or 'tragic' interpretation, was endorsed by Hegel (in his *Lectures on the History of Philosophy*, 1832–3) and further developed by scholars of the calibre of Eduard Zeller (fifth edition 1923), Wilhelm Nestle (1922), and Mario Untersteiner (1954). The second interpretation, which we might describe as the 'empiricist' interpretation, comes from the British liberal milieu and was mostly upheld in Britain by scholars ranging from George Grote (1864) to William Guthrie (1971) and Eric Dodds (1973). Unlike the nihilist interpretations, the 'tragic' one quite rightly emphasizes Gorgias' main aim, namely the highlighting of the fracture between reality and human beings: to paraphrase Untersteiner, there is a tragic antithesis between our impressions and the world that surrounds us, a gap that cannot be bridged because we can only rely on language and know reality through language, and language is deceptive. The result is that each human being is confined within the prison of his or her language and does not entertain any rational (or rather 'logical', bearing in mind what Gorgias means by *logos*) relationship with reality. As far as the experience of *logos* is concerned, the contradictory nature of reality is unsolvable (see also 82B26 D.-K. = 32D34 L.-M.). It is only through an irrational act of volition that we can escape from this prison, so as to adapt ourselves to the multiplicity of reality. The 'empiricist' interpretation, by contrast, emphasizes another fundamental aspect of Gorgias' treatise, namely the centrality of its anti-metaphysical polemic. The result is a completely different picture of Gorgias, whose attack on the Presocratics' metaphysical doctrines is interpreted as an initial defence of the empirical world of common sense. Gorgias thus emerges as a leading exponent of the fifth-century Enlightenment, engaged in a struggle to defend human rationality. Reality exists and we can know it through our senses and via correct reasoning, with no need to yield to the abstract truths of philosophy.

No doubt, these interpretations have the merit of identifying some of the key aspects of Gorgias' thought, from his interest in the problem of language to his focus on logical arguments. However, both of them risk assigning too much to Gorgias: for – and this is a crucial point – what authorizes us to take everything that Gorgias says as his own personal doctrine? On the contrary, what clearly emerges from a reading of his treatise is a dialectical position:[44] his arguments appear to reflect a desire to show to what absurd conclusions the theses or beliefs of his opponents lead, and not to convey any personal theories; Gorgias is arguing *against*, not in *defence of*. In other words, his treatise constitutes an apparently playful reflection on a series of far from playful problems in human life. Yet, we are not justified in turning these reflections and the arguments developed by Gorgias into a holistic theory, as the aforementioned scholars have sought to do. Gorgias' aim is to invite his interlocutors to acknowledge the complexity of these problems, and to challenge them to come up with the most satisfactory solutions. We know nothing at all of his own answers, assuming that he had any to offer: 'There isn't any difficulty in appreciating Gorgias' arguments, once we see them *dialectically* – once, that is, we stop thinking that the only way to be serious is to be dogmatic.'[45] It is essential to clarify this point in order to appreciate Gorgias' teaching. His whole reflection takes the form of an all-out attack against the foundationalist claims of philosophy and common sense: what Gorgias questions is not so much reality itself, as the foundationalist claim that reality possesses some invariant structures and that humans are capable of discerning and communicating such structures.[46] Whether the target is Parmenides or the 'two-headed men', the polemical aim is this alleged correspondence between being, thought, and language, along with everything which this thesis implies: (1) the belief that reality is something ontologically, logically, and temporally independent of us; (2) the idea that knowledge coincides with the objective apprehension

[44] This is suggested, e.g., by Striker 1996: 11–14; Woodruff 1999: 305–6; Caston 2002: 207–8. See also Wardy 1996: 9–24.

[45] Caston 2002: 208.

[46] The main champions of this thesis are Mourelatos 1985, Wardy 1996, and Consigny 2001: 60–73 *et passim*. Cassin 1995 adopts a similar position, with a markedly idiosyncratic reading.

of this independent structure; and (3) trust in the fact that the purpose of language is simply to convey this knowledge.

But – Gorgias asks – are things really so? Can we really speak of an isolated reality, removed from the contingencies of human culture and language? And even assuming that an independent reality exists, does knowledge simply coincide with the correspondence of thought to things? Rather, is it not the case that our opinions, prejudices, expectations, and desires condition our approach to reality? Ultimately, these are the problems that Gorgias is most concerned with. They are substantial problems.

Finally, the anti-foundationalist interpretation just outlined has the merit of explaining what is probably Gorgias' chief contribution, namely his acknowledgement of the importance of language in human experience. As already noted, his whole treatise highlights the complexity of the linguistic phenomenon, and this awareness – as we shall see – also finds significant parallels in the other surviving works by the same author. What makes Gorgias' reflections so interesting is the fact that he freed language (and *logos* more generally) from all ontological implications, all alleged metaphysical correspondences with reality: *logos* is not a reflection of things or the natural means by which to objectively and impartially describe reality.[47] On the contrary, Gorgias asserts the independence of discourse, with its limits and potential. As we shall see, a more in-depth investigation of this problem reveals that his theses constitute a genuine challenge to philosophy.

Two testimonies in the wake of Gorgias' discussion: Xeniades and Lycophron

Gorgias' theses may fruitfully be compared with the thought of another two sophists, Xeniades and Lycophron. Regrettably, little is known about them. According to the sceptic Sextus Empiricus, Xeniades claimed that 'all things are false, that every representation and opinion is false, that everything that comes to be comes to be out of what-is-not, and everything that perishes perishes into what is not' (81.1 D.-K. = 39D1 L.-M.). The emphasis on the theme of not-being and on the limits of human knowledge constitutes a polemical allusion to Parmenides[48] and is reminiscent of Gorgias, if only in a distorted

[47] Segal 1962: 110.
[48] Brunschwig 2002.

way, since it misinterprets the latter's underlying intentions: whereas for Gorgias the analysis of reality is preliminary to that of knowledge and language, here the movement would appear to be in the opposite direction and the outcome is a flight into nothingness. However, it is easy to dismiss this radical position: if nothing *is* and everything is false, then even the thesis according to which nothing *is* and everything is false is false.[49]

More interesting is the case of Lycophron, whom Aristotle in some cases associates with Gorgias and Alcidamas. In a passage of the *Physics* discussing the problematic relation between unity and multiplicity, Aristotle writes:

> Among the ancient thinkers, those who were later [*sc.* than Parmenides and Melissus] were also troubled by the question of knowing how to avoid that the same thing be at the same time one and many of them. That is why some of them suppressed the word 'is', like Lycophron, whereas others changed the mode of expression and said 'the man has been whitened' instead of 'is white'...in order not to make the one be many by adding the word 'is'. (83.2 D.-K. = 38D1 L.-M.)

Lycophron's aim was apparently to offer a solution to the problem of being, which had been the underlying focus of Gorgias' polemic against Parmenides. In fact, Lycophron's suggestion is less radical than what the above passage seems to suggest: a comparison with other, later testimonies from the Neoplatonist commentators of Aristotle shows that, in order to resolve the ambiguities associated with the double use of the verb 'to be', Lycophron suggested that we abolish only the predicative meaning of the verb, and not the existential.[50] 'To be' is only used in the sense of 'to exist', while its copulative use is replaced by concrete verbs. This thesis, however, is not an isolated claim, but may be traced back to an empiricist theory of knowledge. Elsewhere, Aristotle reports that, according to Lycophron, knowledge is constituted of the 'communion' of the act of knowing and the soul (83.1 D.-K. = 38D2 L.-M.): knowledge is not limited to the statement that Socrates is white, but rather extends to the concrete, first-hand experience of Socrates' whiteness.[51] Although this thesis, too, does not necessarily correspond with

[49] Pradeau 2009b: 327.

[50] See Themistius, *Paraphrase of Metaphysics*, 6.25–7.2; Philoponus, *Commentary on Physics*, 43.9–13; Simplicius, *Commentary on Physics*, 93.29–30 (these passages are not included in the D.-K. edition). It seems that a passage from Plato's *Sophist* (251b) can also be traced back to discussions of this kind, albeit not necessarily to Lycophron.

[51] Bonazzi and Pradeau 2009: 335.

Gorgias' positions, it may be read as following in the wake of an anti-Eleatic polemic. It also shows some interesting points of convergence with the ideas of Antisthenes, who, while famously close to Socrates, had been a pupil of Gorgias' as well.[52] Be that as it may, without going too far in the interpretation of such fragmentary testimonies, it is important to note that, for Lycophron, the discussion on reality and being leads to the problem of language: unlike Xeniades, he appears to have grasped the meaning of Gorgias' lesson.

Reality according to Antiphon

Antiphon was certainly among the most prominent sophists, and arguably one of the most fascinating. However, two obstacles have hampered the full appreciation of his merits, unjustly removing him from the centre stage. The first is the problem of his identity, which has added to the complexity of interpreting his ethical and political fragments. A second and just as insidious hindrance has been the prejudice according to which the sophists were only interested in the human world, which is to say rhetorical and political problems. Thus the many fragments of Antiphon's writings that deal with cosmological, biological, meteorological, geometrical, and medical topics have been neglected, in the belief that they constitute a confused mass of information collected from disparate sources. No doubt, Antiphon's analyses are largely indebted to the research conducted by natural philosophers such as Anaxagoras and Democritus or by the Hippocratic physicians. However, the conclusions drawn by Antiphon are far from obvious or banal: on the contrary, the picture of *physis*, of reality, that emerges from his writing is highly original and, as we shall see, constitutes the foundation for even more interesting political considerations. The case of Antiphon also shows that there is no radical break between the sophists and the Presocratic natural philosophers: in their analyses, the sophists did not overlook their predecessors' theses.

Antiphon's main work was entitled *Truth*. This title was not randomly chosen, since it perfectly reflects the context in which its author sought to operate. The title is also significant in relation to Protagoras, since Antiphon's theses, particularly in the political sphere, are very much indebted to and react against the work of the sophist of

[52] See Diogenes Laertius, 6.1; Guthrie 1971: 216–18.

Abdera. One focus of the treatise – perhaps the chief focus – was *physis*, which was investigated from a wide range of perspectives. The most stimulating, and best-known, section of the work concerns human nature; but the author's analysis of humankind was based on a more general analysis of reality, fragments of which also survive.

The following testimony from Aristotle helps clarify the possible meaning of Antiphon's position:

> Some people think that the nature and substance of the things that are by nature is what is present first of all in each thing, without possessing configuration (*arrhuthmistos*) in itself, as the nature of a bed is the wood, and that of a statue the bronze. Antiphon says that evidence of this is the fact that if one were to bury a bed and the rotting could acquire the power of sending up a shoot, it would not become a bed, but wood, which shows that the arrangement in accordance with the rules of the art is merely an accidental attribute, whereas the substance is the other, which, further, persists continuously through the process.
>
> (87B15 D.-K. = partially reproduced in 37D8 L.-M.)

The above claim is far less banal than it seems. The passage establishes an opposition between what – using the Aristotelian terminology – we might call accidental characteristics, and what truly counts, namely the essence, that which subsists continuously. This opposition between convention and reality, couched in terms of the opposition between *nomos* and *physis*, was to play a decisive role in Antiphon's thought. Here it is interesting to note the way in which *physis*, understood as the ultimate material constituent, is presented: according to Aristotle's testimony, the term which Antiphon used to describe nature is *arrythmiston*, 'without configuration', a rare adjective that may be traced back to the Democritean tradition. *Physis*, then, is the unconfigured material substrate that resists all external attempts to lend it order.[53] Other fragments too – unfortunately, very short ones – confirm this picture (87B10, 12, 22–5 D.-K. = 37D9, 37, 18–21 L.-M.), suggesting that Antiphon championed an organic, dynamic, and materialist view of reality. *Physis* is something living and ever-changing that obeys its own rhythm, not one imposed from the outside: the natural constituents of the universe (such as the sun and planets) are the product of a chain of causal relations which do not stem from any intelligent or finalistic plan, but only from the accidental combination of the elements (87B28–32 D.-K. = 37D24–7 L.-M.).

[53] See Romeyer-Dherbey 1985: 96–103.

The implications of these views are far from negligible, when examined against the background of their cultural context: Antiphon's defence of the idea of a universe governed by necessity but not providence reflects an attempt on his part to clearly distance himself from all mythical or religious explanations of reality. Moreover, he distances himself not just from religious traditions but also from most of the Presocratics, who – while emancipating themselves from the world of myth – had assigned the ultimate principle or principles a series of positive attributes usually assigned to the gods: for Antiphon, the nature of the all is not divine. Finally, from the opposite perspective, we cannot rule out a criticism of Protagoras and Gorgias, who, by placing humans at the centre of everything, had denied the priority of *physis*. Antiphon succeeds in the delicate task of striking a middle ground, emphasizing the centrality of nature while at the same time denying any axiological superiority to this priority: his nature, true reality, is something neutral, devoid of any meaning or value that might direct human choices. Reality is indifferent: the importance of these theses will become clear once the discussion focuses on humankind.[54]

Someone who had fully realized the significance of the kind of theses put forward by Antiphon was Plato, who in the *Laws* – which is to say in the last years of his life, at a fair distance from the debates and cultural climate of the fifth century – felt the need to newly address the same problems in order to decry their dangers. In Book 10, the Athenian Stranger sets out to inform his two friends, the Spartan Megillus and the Cretan Clinias, about those theses which were then circulating in Athens concerning nature and the gods. Although the thinkers referred to by Plato are unnamed, it is more than likely that, among others, he was targeting Anaxagoras (who had denied the divine nature of the sun, arguing that it was only a fiery rock – a thesis at the root of all problems: 886d–e), Democritus, and even Antiphon. The last, as has been suggested, may in fact be Plato's chief polemical target.[55]

The thesis put forward by the anonymous thinkers is that the universe is the necessary outcome of the accidental combination of its material constituents, which 'moved at random, each impelled by virtue of its own inherent properties' (889b). While the combination of necessity and chance, two apparently contrasting concepts, may seem odd at

[54] See Gagarin 2002: 69–71.

[55] Untersteiner 1949–62: iv.178–95; Decleva Caizzi 1986a; Neschke Hentske 1995: 140–9; Bonazzi 2012. See also Sedley 2013.

first, it reveals an interesting idea, which confirms the Antiphontic tone of the passage. What is meant by chance (*tyche*) is not a blind or irrational force, but an order of things which does not depend on transcendent forces or intelligent designs, but on the intrinsic features of its constituents. Once the theory has been reconstructed in these terms (it is not that far from modern theories, one may note), the reasons for Plato's opposition become clear: what we have is a first attempt to explain reality in merely materialistic and mechanistic terms, an explanation that – should it prove convincing – would entail the negation of the existence of the divine ('the gods exist. . .not by nature, but by certain legal conventions', 889e) and hence of all providentialism and finalism. This, in turn, would amount to the negation of values such as justice and virtue, which were traditionally associated with the divine order of reality. The result, in one word, is atheism; and atheism, according to Plato, is the greatest ill of all, on account of its political consequences: with the disappearance of the gods, the values of justice and morality safeguarded by the gods also vanish ('there is no natural standard of justice at all. On the contrary, men are always wrangling about their moral standards and altering them', 889e). The only remaining law, then, is that of violence: 'everything one can get away with by force is absolutely justified'; 'the true [note the importance of this term] natural life is essentially nothing but a life of conquest over others, not one of service to your neighbour as the law enjoins'; and this justifies those acts of impiety and subversion which have driven Athens and the Greek world to the verge of the abyss (890a–b; cf. 715a–716c).

As we shall see in the following chapters, it is most unlikely that Antiphon advocated violence: the link between an independent conception of nature, atheism, and political violence is something inferred by Plato, who finds in this connection further confirmation of his view that the sophists' teaching is a social threat. Still, the fact remains that Antiphon's theses posed a radical challenge to intellectual traditions that were well rooted in the Greek world. And, in this respect, Antiphon proves himself to be a fine sophist.

From *physis* to *logos*: Presocratics and sophists

In the light of the analyses conducted thus far, it is possible to redefine the sophists' position vis-à-vis the Presocratic philosophers. No less simplistic than the claim that the Presocratics focused only on the natural world and not on the human world is the thesis that the sophists had no interest in *physis* and only focused on humanity. Rather, what the sophists appear to have polemically engaged with is the fascination with what is obscure, with the hidden nature of things.[56] However, *physis* as such remains the starting point of all enquiries. To be more precise, reality remains the central problem that cannot be overlooked: the common denominator in all these disparate theories, often developed in polemical contrast to one another, is the acknowledgement of the problematic nature of reality.[57]

And yet, the sophists are responsible for a fundamental turn in the history of philosophy, a turn the importance of which can hardly be ignored: a shift of focus from nature to the human world. Of course, as has been noted, this does not mean that the Presocratics had not focused on the human world; but they had done so starting from their study of *physis*, by considering human beings as part of the whole. The sophists adopted a completely new perspective, by setting out from the belief that things must be turned round, that it is reductive to consider humans simply as a part of the whole. On the contrary, in their view it is necessary to set out from human beings and their uniqueness with respect to other entities. In other words, the sophists follow in the trail of the Presocratic philosophical tradition and continue to investigate problems related to nature, the city, and humankind, but following an opposite hierarchy, based on a decisive philosophical intuition that no subsequent thinkers could afford to ignore: the idea that the relation between reality and human beings is problematic and cannot be taken for granted, but must rather be constructed. And it is on the basis of this acknowledgement that the sophists discussed human beings and their problems: for if nature in itself is ambiguous, neutral, or devoid of meaning, one must turn elsewhere in order to discover the meaning of humanity's experience and life. The attention shifts from cosmology to epistemology, from the study of reality in itself to that of how we can know reality and relate to it – from *physis* to *logos*.

[56] Woodruff 1999: 309.
[57] Paci 1957: 126.

III A WORLD OF WORDS: THE SOPHISTS AT THE CROSSROADS BETWEEN GRAMMAR, RHETORIC, POETRY, AND PHILOSOPHY

An interest in speech and an admiration for those capable of speaking well was a recurrent feature of the Greek world from its most archaic period. Contrary to a certain stereotyped image, the Homeric hero is not celebrated only for his strength and beauty; his ability to express himself is also fundamental: Achilles is the most famous hero, and Phoenix's duty was to teach him how to be 'both a speaker of words and a doer of deeds' (*Iliad*, 9.442–3). In times of war and peace, authority largely depended on one's skill in rhetoric, which allowed one to settle disputes and provide suitable advice (see, for example, Hesiod, *Theogony*, 83–7).[1] Later on, the development of the institution of the *polis* further increased the importance of this skill, which became even more crucial in Athenian democracy, in an age in which courtrooms and assemblies shaped men's lives and careers. Hence the sophists' success, which reflects the fame they enjoyed as masters of the art of speech: it is because he 'makes you a clever speaker' that the young Hippocrates wishes to rush off to visit Protagoras in Plato's dialogue of the same name (*Protagoras*, 312d–e).

The sophists, in other words, are specialists in *logos*, in all the senses encompassed by this term: *logos* may refer to the whole field of language and words as much as that of arguments, thoughts, and mental processes.[2] The sophists asserted their competence in all of these domains, and not just from a practical perspective; their reflection provided the foundation for their investigation even from a theoretical point of view: with the sophists, language and arguments became a privileged matter of debate. Our sources inform us that they investigated these problems from all angles, with a truly remarkable breadth of perspective and competence. To be more precise, we can demarcate three specific areas that bear witness to their interest in *logos*: grammar and the issue of the correctness of names; the criticism of and engagement with poetry; and rhetoric and the effectiveness of argumentative techniques. In all these fields, the sophists earned indisputable prestige, as Plato was to acknowledge in the *Cratylus*: to learn about these matters,

[1] Pernot 2006: 15–22.
[2] Gagarin 2008.

Socrates observes, 'the most correct way is to investigate together with people who already know, but you must pay them well and show gratitude besides – those are the sophists' (*Cratylus*, 391b).

Grammar and the correctness of names

Many sources bear witness to the sophists' interest in grammar. This applies especially to Protagoras, who focused on morphological, syntactic, and stylistic questions: apparently, he was the first to distinguish the gender of nouns (male, female, and neuter), while also suggesting many corrections for names in use in his day. Thus he suggested that the female nouns *menis* ('wrath', 'frenzy') and *pelex* ('helmet'), two terms familiar to Homer's audience, should be regarded as masculine – either on the basis of morphological criteria (because names ending in sigma or xi are usually masculine) or because of their meaning (insofar as war is an eminently masculine pursuit: see 80A27–8 D.-K. = 31D23–4 L.-M.). Protagoras also distinguished four verbal modes (indicative, conjunctive, optative, and imperative), which he linked to four types of speech (prayer, question, reply, and command), once again taking the occasion to criticize Homer, who had addressed the goddess with a command ('Sing, Goddess, the wrath') rather than a prayer (80A29 D.-K. = 31D25 L.-M.). Ultimately, these grammatical reflections presuppose a sophisticated conception of language, which is not limited to names but is rather investigated from the point of view of its underlying structure and connections, in relation to the different functions of terms.[3] As further confirmation of the importance of this research, it should be added that Protagoras was not the only sophist to deal with these problems: Hippias investigated the rhythms, harmonies, and correctness of letters (86A12 D.-K. = 36D15 L.-M), and Alcidamas proposed an alternative division of the types of speech from Protagoras' (affirmation, negation, question, and address: fr. 24 Patillon with Mazzara 2005). The coining of neologisms can probably be traced back to the same context as well (Antiphon and Critias appear to have been particularly keen on inventing new terms, a remarkable number of which survive).

Naturally, it would be a serious mistake to assume that this focus on language depended on exclusively erudite or grammatical interests, as

[3] Brancacci 1996: 116–17.

though the sophists simply sought to codify or standardize the linguistic usages of the Greek world. On the contrary, practical and philosophical interests were in play. On the one hand, it was a matter of increasing the potential of words in view of the practical aim of teaching pupils to exploit language to further their goals: it is by mastering a language that one can use it more effectively.[4] As Aristophanes was to note, these are the tools that help 'to make the weaker argument the stronger' (80B6b D.-K.): in order to learn the 'unjust argument' (Aristophanes' version of Protagoras' 'weaker argument'), one must first learn the rules of grammar (*Clouds*, 658–91 = 80C3 D.-K. = Dram. T19c L.-M.).

On the other hand, it should be noted that the issues discussed by the sophists raised some important theoretical questions. One recurrent focus of their research was the issue of the correctness of names (*orthotes onomaton*, *orthoepeia*[5]), which is to say the capacity of language to faithfully portray reality: this kind of enquiry is what contributed to early philosophical reflection on the nature of language.[6] The correctness of names no doubt represents one of the problems most widely debated in the Greek world, and not just by sophists, either: let us think here of figures such as Democritus and Antisthenes, not to mention Plato's *Cratylus*, whose subtitle was 'On the Correctness of Names'.

Among the sophists, the most interesting reflections were made by Protagoras and Prodicus. The latter's investigation of the correctness of names took the form of a detailed analysis of synonyms, which earned him great repute among the men of his day. By first grouping synonyms together and then distinguishing them, Prodicus sought to connect each name to its concrete reality.[7] His theory presupposes a one-to-one relation between words and their referents, such that the phenomenon of synonymity seems only apparent. Prodicus thus emerges as a forerunner of Socrates' theories (significantly, the sources

[4] Classen 1976: 223–5.

[5] The distinction between these two expressions is unclear: see Guthrie 1971: 205.

[6] Guthrie 1971: 220.

[7] Momigliano 1930. It is difficult to determine on what basis Prodicus drew his distinctions: in some cases he would appear to rely on the traditional use of terms (e.g. 84A18 D.-K., partially reproduced in 34D24 L.-M.), while elsewhere he seems to suggest radical innovations based on their etymology (84B4 D.-K. = 34D9 L.-M.; see Pfeiffer 1968: 40–1). The small number of testimonies makes it difficult to come up with a definite answer to these questions: see Classen 1976: 232–7. As rightly noted by Dorion 2009b: 531 n. 22 in relation to 84A16 D.-K., Prodicus also investigated the problem of homonymy, which is to say the phenomenon of the semantic ambiguity of a term (the term in this particular case being *manthano*, which in Greek means both 'to understand' and 'to learn').

often associate the two[8]), the main difference being that, whereas Prodicus appear to proceed by asking 'how does x differ from y', Socrates focuses more directly on individual entities, asking 'what is x?'[9] In Prodicus' case, this interest in names and synonyms has favoured a particular interpretation of his thought, which has emphasized his specificity compared to other sophists. It has been noted that his distinctions usually (but not always: see 84B4 D.-K. = 34D9 L.-M.) refer to terms and concepts pertaining to the field of ethics or moral psychology.[10] This has led some scholars to set Prodicus in contrast 'to people the likes of Callicles and Thrasymachus', as an opponent of the relativism typical of these authors and the upholder of a certain foundation for the moral principles that are to govern people's lives.[11] Provided that we bear in mind the rhetorical purposes of this kind of research in Prodicus' case as well, the reconstruction in question is largely valid (we will be returning to it in Chapter 5).[12] Prodicus' positive ethical orientation, however, does not entail such a radical contrast with the other sophists, as may be inferred from a comparison with Protagoras.

Plato's *Phaedrus* suggests that one of Protagoras' works was entitled *Orthoepeia* (*The Correctness of Language*; *Phdr.* 267c = 80A26 D.-K. = 31D22a L.-M.). Regrettably, the content of this book is completely unknown; but different sources confirm that Protagoras had an interest in the problem of the correctness of language at different levels.[13] Mention has already been made of Protagoras' grammatical interests and criticism of Homer, which implied the thesis of linguistic correctness. On another level, the notion of *orthos* is used as a criterion of analysis for poetry: correctness in this case concerns not points of grammar, but the consistency of a composition, its statements, and its moral teaching (80A25 D.-K. = 31D31 and 42 L.-M.; we will be returning to this testimony in the following section). Finally, the same notion could also be applied in an even more general sense:

[8] See Guthrie 1971: 275.

[9] Classen 1976: 232.

[10] Dumont 1986; Wolfsdorf 2008b.

[11] In this respect, it is interesting to note that, in the *Euthydemus*, Plato mentions Prodicus twice as a potential opponent of sophists and eristic debaters such as Euthydemus and Dionysodorus: see *Euth.* 277e and 305c.

[12] Cole 1991: 100.

[13] Gagarin 2008: 28–30. More in general, see Rademaker 2013.

When a competitor in the pentathlon unintentionally struck Epitimus of Pharsalus with a javelin and killed him, he [i.e. Pericles] spent a whole day with Protagoras examining the difficulty whether, according to the *most correct reasoning*, it was the javelin, or the man who threw it, or the umpires, that should be considered responsible for this unfortunate event.

(80A10 D.-K. = 31D30 L.-M.)

This testimony is a fine example of Protagoras' way of reasoning. The facts are indisputable: a man has unintentionally killed another man.[14] However, much remains to be said in regard to the issues of moral responsibility, legal guilt, and how to judge the whole incident. One and the same indisputable fact may be viewed from many different perspectives: for the physician, the javelin will be responsible for the man's death; for the judge, it will be the javelin-thrower; for the person who has organized the competition, it will be the judge. This contrast gives the sophist some room for action: he will attempt to create some agreement, lending meaning and order to the event.[15] The notion of correctness is the criterion which enables him to overcome the above difficulties: given that there is some truth and validity to all the above points of view, the problem will be to find the one most suited to the situation, while foregoing any claim to come up with a single, abstract answer.[16]

The notion of 'correctness' finds a prominent place in Protagoras' thought, and allows us to grasp some of its strands of continuity.[17] At the basis of this notion lies the awareness of the problematic relationship between reality and the human world which we discussed in connection with the 'man-measure' thesis, and which finds another expression in the statement that 'concerning every subject, there are

[14] Significantly, Antiphon's second *Tetralogy* discusses the same problem. See also Antiphon's fr. 87B44, 4.10 (= 37D38 L.-M.), where the criterion of 'correct reasoning' is used to establish what causes pain and what pleasure. Another interesting occurrence of the criterion of correctness is to be found in the *Encomium of Helen*, where Gorgias sets out 'to say correctly what is necessary' in order to preserve Helen's honour (82B11, 2 D.-K. = 32D24 L.-M.).

[15] Untersteiner 1954: 30–2 and 66.

[16] Gagarin 2008: 30.

[17] This doctrine also shows that Protagoras was not endorsing a conventionalist theory of names, as one might well expect (see Pl. *Crat.* 391b–d and the observations rightly made by Corradi 2006: 54–5). A conventionalist position is possibly to be found in Euthydemus and Dionysodorus' thesis, as presented in Plato's *Euthydemus*, and has also been attributed to Antiphon by Guthrie 1971: 204 on the basis of the pseudo-Hippocratic treatise *On Art* that Diels published as an appendix to 87B1 D.-K. (= Med. T2 L.-M.). In this passage, however, the author's silence as regards his polemical aims makes it difficult to prove Guthrie's thesis. In the same period, in close proximity to the sophists, Democritus appears to have upheld a similarly conventionalist thesis: see Barnes 1979: i.164–9.

two arguments opposed to one another' (80B6a D.-K. = 31D26 L.-M.). With regard to each thing there are two opposite *logoi* (speeches, arguments, points of view) – A and not-A – precisely because each experience is open to contrasting readings and interpretations. *Logos*, which expresses our capacity to think and speak, thus cannot exhaust the complexity of reality.[18] However, as already noted with regard to the 'man-measure' thesis, contradictory points of view do not imply confusion or the failure of human possibilities. Rather, the challenge that Protagoras takes up and the promise he makes is to be able to (and teach others to) unravel this complexity by identifying which of any two opposite *logoi* is the better, or rather the more correct, which is to say the one better suited to the circumstance at hand: this is the meaning of his well-known claim to 'to make the weaker argument the stronger' (80B6b D.-K.). It is easy to discern the structural analysis that links this notion of correctness to that of the type of usefulness we have discussed in relation to the 'man-measure' fragment: in both cases the problem is to find the best, most expedient relationship with things in each circumstance. We here get a better idea of Protagoras' teaching, which centres on the concept of *logos*, understood both as the ability to reason and the ability to express oneself (that is, as both thought and language[19]). 'Correctness', in other words, is to be understood on two levels, one conceptual and the other linguistic: correct reasoning, which expresses the best possible solution, must find a counterpart in formal correctness, which makes one's speech persuasive and hence allows one to gain the upper hand in each particular situation.[20] The best speech, therefore, is not the speech that is true but the one that is correct, the speech best suited to the situation at hand and most capable of outdoing others from a formal and logical perspective: an irrefutable *logos*.[21]

The notion of 'correct' thus encapsulates the two underlying motivations of Protagoras' thought: on the one hand, the concrete need to win discussions and debates; on the other, a more profound reflection on

[18] The same conception also explains the statement that 'it is not possible to contradict' (80A19 D.-K. = 31R 10 L.-M.): to the extent that each individual entertains a relationship with things whose reality and truth cannot be disputed or contradicted, the opposition here is only apparent. It is interesting to note that in a recently republished papyrus, the same thesis is also attributed to Prodicus, only on the basis of different arguments: see PToura III 16, 9–18, reprinted in Bonazzi 2007: 261 (= 34R14 L.-M.).

[19] See Corradi 2007b.

[20] Classen 1976: 222–5.

[21] Brancacci 2002b: 183–90.

the human beings and the importance of *logos*, understood as the capacity to reason and to express oneself – as thought and speech. An increased awareness of the chasm between human beings and reality goes hand in hand with a belief that, through *logos*, humans can become the measure of all things. This is what Protagoras' thesis ultimately amounts to, and it is easy to see that Prodicus and the other sophists had reached the same conclusion, by different routes.

Literary criticism and the critique of the poetic tradition

In the Platonic dialogue of the same name, Protagoras, when illustrating the aims of his teaching, assigns a particularly central place to poetry:

> I think. . .that for a man the most important part of education consists in being expert concerning poems; and this means to be able to understand what is said correctly by the poets and what is not. (Plato, *Protagoras*, 338e–339a = 80A25 D.-K. = 31D31 L.-M.)

An interest in language did not merely inspire grammatical investigations and pave the way for rhetoric: it also constituted a privileged means to engage with the poetic tradition. Literary criticism first emerged in this period, also thanks to the sophists' contributions. Yet this is not all. Poets had traditionally been regarded as educators and as the custodians of the most genuine Greek tradition: poetry was a treasure trove of useful knowledge, an encyclopaedia of ethics, politics, and history that every good citizen was expected to assimilate as the core of his education. The poet's task was to preserve and transmit the system of values on which the life of his community was founded. To engage with poetry, therefore, was to engage with the tradition; and this engagement was a fundamental part of the sophists' teaching. Generally speaking, the rhapsodes were the social figures entrusted with the transmission of the poets' knowledge. By declaiming the Homeric poems, they contributed to spreading a whole cultural heritage, consisting of norms and values. The rhapsodes did not merely recite verses: they also commented on them, and in doing so, they imparted teachings and instructions (see Plato, *Ion*, 530c–d). By developing different reading strategies, which often went against the established ones, the sophists presented themselves as the heirs to the rhapsodes, in some cases even donning their garb (e.g. Gorgias and Hippias: see 82A9

D.-K. = 32P18 L.-M.). In such a way, the sophists reinforced their claim to be new teachers, educators capable of imparting teachings suited to the needs of the new world of the *polis*.[22] The sophists' strategy is one of appropriation, where an engagement with traditional knowledge represents the starting point of their attempt to acquire a dominant position in the Athenian cultural scene.[23]

The aforementioned evidence from Protagoras is very clear in this respect. In the dialogue, the above claim is followed by the reading of a poem by Simonides, one of the great lyric poets of the Greek world, with the declared aim of highlighting its incongruities and contradictions with respect to questions such as virtue and the good. Once again, the criterion used for this analysis is that of 'correctness'. Protagoras follows a specific method, that of literal interpretation, which unfolds in three successive stages (understanding, analysing, and giving account). This method brings together all the various aspects of the research on language conducted by Protagoras:

> [1] the study and examination of the poetic text governed by the criterion of *orthotes*; [2] the analysis of the poetic text from a grammatical, verbal, and logical perspective; [3] explanation and discussion of the text itself, to the point of turning it into the subject matter of the dialectical conversation.[24]

Clearly, the purpose is not to provide a mere exegesis. Rather, it is to critically discuss the text and fulfil an educational goal: literary criticism is a useful intellectual exercise which enables the individual to

[22] See Pfeiffer 1968: 16–17; Soverini 1998: 6–12. Very interesting reflections are also to be found in Most 1986, who stresses the importance of the interpretation of literary texts as a distinctive feature of the sophists. Indeed, the sophists' penchant for the written word constitutes a distinguishing element with respect to the oral culture in which poets found themselves operating: see again Pfeiffer 1968: 24–30. It is worth recalling the fact that several sophists were also the authors of poetical works: this is the case with Hippias (86A12 and B1 D.-K. = 36D2 and D4 L.-M.), Critias, and possibly Antiphon (see 87A6 a 9 D.-K. = 37P8 L.-M.).

[23] Goldhill 1986: 222–43; Morgan 2000: 89–94.

[24] Brancacci 1996: 111. The likely polemical target of this method of literal exegesis is the allegorical exegesis developed by Theagenes of Rhegium in the sixth century BC and later taken up in Athens by another great intellectual of the period, Anaxagoras of Clazomenae, and by his pupil Metrodorus of Lampsacus (on these authors, see Rocca-Serra 1990 and Morgan 2000: 98–101). Evidence of a polemic between Protagoras and the champions of the allegorical method is possibly to be found in testimony 80A30 D.-K. (= 31D32 L.-M.), in which Protagoras focuses on a theomachy, a theme dear to Homeric interpreters of the allegorical tradition (who were wont to interpret theomachies as symbolizing the oppositions between natural elements, such as hot and cold, or dry and moist): see Brancacci 1996: 118. On Protagoras and Homer see, more recently, Capra 2005 and Corradi 2006: 56–63.

grow familiar with the works of the poets and hence with traditional values – values that the individual will then be free to engage with, by either approving or rejecting them.[25] Similar conclusions are suggested by other sources I have mentioned, namely the (regrettably) very succinct texts in which Protagoras analyses and criticizes some Homeric verses (80A28–30 D.-K. = 31D24–5, 30 L.-M.): by showing his ability to discuss the great Homer, while at the same time taking the liberty of criticizing him, Protagoras justifies his claim to be the new teacher that the city needs.

The importance of an engagement with the poetic tradition finds confirmation that is only apparently unexpected in the 'man-measure' fragment. In the previous chapter we saw how one of Protagoras' polemical targets was Parmenides and the philosophical tradition of the 'teachers of the truth'. Yet these were not the only 'teachers of the truth' attacked by the sophists, since much the same holds true of the poets, who had often drawn upon the idea of 'measure' to assert their importance: a poet – to quote some famous verses – is someone who, by grace of the Muses, knows the 'measure' of loving wisdom (Solon, fr. 1, 51–2 Gentili-Prato) and possesses the 'measure' of wisdom (Theognis, 873–6).[26] A poet, in other words, is someone who, by virtue of the divine protection he enjoys, is capable of speaking the truth and distinguishing it from falsehood; he is the custodian of the order of reality and this justifies his prominent role in society.[27] Everything changes with Protagoras: the 'man-measure' thesis undermines the poets' claim to truth, just as it does with the truth referred to by philosophers such as Parmenides (who ultimately were operating within the same context as the tradition of poetic lore: he too wrote in verse). The truth is no longer guaranteed by gods and inspired poets, since humans are now the measure of all things, each according to their own perspective. And Protagoras is the new teacher, and the only one who can help others find their bearings in the ambiguous world that surrounds them, in which contrasting opinions take the place of absolute truth and falsehood. We can thus appreciate the programmatic importance of Protagoras' introductory speech at the beginning of Plato's *Protagoras*, where he proclaims himself to be the heir to an authoritative, centuries-old tradition:

[25] Morgan 2000: 94.
[26] See Corradi 2007a.
[27] Arrighetti 1998: xv–xxi; Detienne 2006: 113–24.

I say that the sophistic art is ancient, but that those ancient men who practiced it, because they feared the annoyance it caused, employed a screen and disguised it, some using poetry, like Homer, Hesiod, and Simonides, and others initiatory rites and oracles, the followers of Orpheus and Musaeus; and certain ones, I have heard, under gymnastic too, like Iccus of Tarentum and another one, still alive, as much a sophist as anyone: Herodicus of Selymbria, originally a Megarian colony. And music was the screen employed by your fellow citizen Agathocles, a great sophist, Pythoclides of Ceos, and many others.[28]

(Pl. *Prot.* 316d–317c)

This claim is not merely designed to place Protagoras under the aegis of a well-rooted tradition; rather, it contributes to a more complex strategy of appropriation, which, through an apparently slavish adherence, brings about a radical reversal.

While Protagoras seems to focus entirely on the rational and rationally analysable aspects of poetic language, Gorgias also shows an interest in its psychagogic and creative aspects (without overlooking the importance of rational arguments, as we will see in the following section). The assumptions and aims, however, are the same: the centrality of *logos* and the ambition to establish oneself as Greece's true teacher. In particular, Gorgias' reflection is marked by an acknowledgement of the power of words and by the notion of deception. In this respect, the most interesting text is his declamation *Encomium of Helen*, which was apparently composed to defend the memory of Homer's famous heroine, guilty of having fled with Paris, bringing about the Trojan War. Among the various reasons that may have led Helen to flee to Troy, Gorgias considers the arguments by which Paris might have persuaded her, and this allows him to embark on a famous digression on the power of *logos* and what constitutes it, namely words:

Speech (*logos*) is a great potentate that by means of an extremely tiny and entirely invisible body performs the most divine deeds. For it is able to stop fear, to remove grief, to instil joy, and to increase pity. (82B11, 8 D.-K. = 32D24, 8 L.-M.)

The acknowledgement of this power of words, a power that is also magical and divine, leads Gorgias to introduce the concept of deception (*apate*), which lies at the basis of his aesthetics.[29]

[28] Only part of this passage is included in the Diels-Kranz edition, as 80A5 D.-K. (the whole text appears in Bonazzi 2009b as T6 and L.-M. as Soph. R11). On its importance, see Brancacci 2002a.

[29] See Rosenmeyer 1955; Verdenius 1981; Horky 2006.

The notion of deceit can probably be traced back to Parmenides, and certainly to the poetic tradition of earlier centuries.[30] In Gorgias, however, it lacks the negative nuance that it possesses in Parmenides and the poets. When Parmenides describes his cosmology as deceptive, he is not saying that it is false or fallacious; rather, he is warning his audience that what they are dealing with is still the world of appearances and not that of true reality. Much the same holds true for the poets. In Gorgias, by contrast, there is no longer any room for a 'true divine reality' beyond the changing world of appearances: all that remains is phenomena and the uncertain opinions of men. The deception stems from this precarious situation: every opinion – which is to say every attempt to make sense of reality – is intrinsically deceitful, since it is incapable of faithfully representing a reality that *cannot* be faithfully represented. But it is evident that in this context deception loses all negative connotations: for such is the human condition. And it is from this situation that poetry and all other forms of art can set out to achieve their goals.

Gorgias provides the first 'aesthetic' reflection on art and its power: the aim of the 'deception' embodied by art is to charm the soul by rousing feelings of pleasure, joy, or pain.[31] Yet, as we have just seen, the triggering of an emotional response is not an end in itself: it is a way to know oneself better and build a relationship with reality, which, according to Gorgias, is always 'other' with respect to us – a way of making sense of ourselves and the things around us. Deception, in other words, is to be fostered because it is what allows us to build a relationship with the reality of things and the reality of our very own being: the problem is not to attain a universal truth but to 'enrich our universe, expanding our knowledge and culture, which is to say our self-understanding, our capacity to explain our own being'.[32] With Gorgias, what we have for the first time is an awareness of the value of art, 'a deception, in which the one who deceives is more just than the one who does not deceive, and the one who is deceived is more intelligent that the one who is not deceived' (82B23 D-K. = 32D35

[30] As regards Parmenides, see fr. 28B, 56 D.-K. (= Parm. 19D8.57 L.-M.) and Verdenius 1981: 124. On the poetic tradition, see de Romilly 1975: 1–22 and de Romilly 1973, who also notes that this conception of poetry as something magical and illusionary (see e.g. 82B11, 9 D.-K. = 32D24, 9 L.-M.) might reflect an influence from Empedocles (whose disciple Gorgias may have been: 82A3, 10 D.-K. = 32P4–5 L.-M., and Kerferd 1985).

[31] Segal 1962: 124.

[32] Casertano 2004: 83

L.-M.).[33] Not unlike Protagoras, however, Gorgias implements a subtle strategy by appropriating traditional poetic lore, as poetry is nothing but 'a speech (*logos*) that possess meter' (82B11, 9 D.-K. = 32D24, 9 L.-M.): what matters, then, is *logos* and the ability to make suitable use of it. The real object of the encomium is not Helen but *logos*.[34] This justifies the subsuming of poetry within the broader genre of rhetoric, the art of *logos* which is the object of Gorgias' teaching: like Protagoras, Gorgias plays with tradition in order to appropriate it.[35] The lore safeguarded by the poet has now been integrated in the wisdom of rhetors and sophists.

Among the other sophists, Hippias stands out for his interest in poetry and traditional lore. We know that he dealt with the division and length of syllables, probably in relation to metrical and rhythmic issues (see 86A2 and 12 D.-K. = 36D14b and 15 L.-M.). Moreover, he was well known in antiquity for his 'antiquarian' interests: that is, for having gathered and catalogued quotes from the great masters of past centuries – poets such as Orpheus, Musaeus, Homer, and Hesiod, among others (86B6 D.-K. = 36D22 L.-M.; Hippias' interest in Homer is also documented elsewhere: see 86A10, 9, 18 D.-K. = 36D25, 26, 24 L.-M.). Hippias' immediate aim, of course, was to provide a series of quotes that could be used in speeches and discussions. However, this work of selection may also be seen to promote a more detached approach to the tradition, which is viewed from a historical perspective and no longer as the depository of unquestionable truths.

This work of critical revision of poetic lore finds further confirmation in the method of memorization (*mnemotechnique*) that made Hippias famous (86A2, 5a, 11–12, 16 D.-K. = 36D12–13 L.-M.). Up until then, memory had served as the poet's key tool: it had exercised a religious function that enabled him to get in touch with divine reality and acquire knowledge of present, past, and future. With Hippias – and indeed Simonides before him – memory becomes a '"secular" technique, a psychological faculty that each person exercises according to well-defined rules, rules that are available to everyone'.[36] This

[33] This idea is also taken up in the *Dissoi logoi*, 89, 3, 10–12 D.-K. (= 40, 3, 10–12 L.-M.), which quotes verses by the poets Cleoboulina and Aeschylus.

[34] Segal 1962: 102; Poulakos 1983.

[35] In Gorgias' case, appropriation also entails an attempt to adapt the poetic style to the kind of prose declamations typical of his oeuvre: see 82A29 D.-K. (= 32D21b L.-M.) and de Romilly 1975: 8–11.

[36] Detienne 2006: 191.

engenders a new attitude to time, regarded not as the 'power of oblivion', but as the context in which human endeavours take place.[37] Hippias thus contributes to the development of historical awareness, and the only surviving authentic passage by him, the aforementioned fragment B6, bears unquestionable witness to the pride that he took in affirming the innovative nature of his teaching:

> Of these [*sc.* probably: ancient opinions] some have doubtless been expressed by Orpheus, others by Musaeus, to put it briefly, by each one in a different place, others by Hesiod, others by Homer, others by the other poets; others in treatises; some by Greeks, others by non-Greeks. But I myself have put together from out of all these the ones that are most important and akin to one another, and on their basis I shall compose the following new and variegated discourse. (86B6 D.-K. = 36D22 L.-M.)[38]

The case of Critias, in contrast, is a more problematic one. Probably following Philostratus' lead, Diels reckoned him among the sophists. Certainly, Critias' interest in antiquarian traditions and poetry finds a parallel in the work of other sophists.[39] However, his ideology seems to follow a radically different direction, insofar as he apparently upholds a return to tradition and poetry (a genre he practised extensively) against the threats posed by the new rhetorical education (see Brisson 2009: 395).[40] The differences here seem far more significant than the points of convergence.[41]

Rhetoric, the sophists, and philosophy

As should be clear by now, the interest in *logos* is central to the sophists' conceptualizations. In the previous section, we examined how the

[37] Detienne 2006: 192.

[38] Besides, it is worth noting that Hippias' 'antiquarian' interests were not limited to poetic quotes, since he also made lists of the winners at the Olympics, so as to establish a reliable chronology of Greek history (86B3 D.-K. = 36D7 L.-M.), of the founding of cities, and of human genealogies (86A2 and B2 D.-K. = 36D14b and D30 L.-M.), and of many other topics pertaining to mythological, ethnographic, geographical, and philosophical traditions (86B6–9, 12 D.-K. = 36D22–3, 26–8 L.-M.). On Hippias' pursuits as a polymath, see Brunschwig 1984; A. Patzer 1986; Pfeiffer 1968: 51–4; Mansfeld 1986; and Balaudé 2006.

[39] Pfeiffer 1968: 54–5.

[40] See Brisson 2009: 395.

[41] Another text that might help us further clarify the nature of the sophists' interest in literary criticism and poetry is an anonymous papyrus (*POxy*. III 414) that Giuliano 1998 has hypothetically assigned to Antiphon. In his collection of fragments of the sophists, moreover, Untersteiner had published an anonymous treatise *On Music*, which deals with similar issues (Untersteiner 1949–62: iii.208–11).

sophists used their new form of knowledge in relation to – and in competition with – the traditional knowledge embodied by poetry. We can now move on to analyse how this interest in *logos* relates to rhetoric, which developed as an independent form of knowledge in the late fifth and early fourth centuries BC. In turn, this will allow us to return to the thorny question of the relation between the sophists and philosophy, an issue which we began to address in the previous chapter.

The extent of the sophists' contribution to rhetoric has been at the centre of a lively debate in recent scholarship. Despite the fact that several sophists were credited with the authorship of textbooks (the so-called *logon technai*), and that Gorgias, Antiphon, and Thrasymachus have traditionally been regarded as the founding fathers of this discipline,[42] some modern scholars have noted that the surviving testimonies seem to suggest that a genuine reflection on this new literary genre only emerged with Plato and Aristotle.[43] The problem is certainly an interesting one, and it is difficult to take a side in the debate, given that the sources we have do not allow us to clearly determine the extent to which the sophists may have contributed to the development of theoretical problems (for example, the classification of different rhetorical genres, such as the deliberative, epideictic, and judicial) or stylistics (for instance, the distinction between high and low style). What is certain is that, although the sophists were not the 'official' founders of rhetoric, they showed an interest in *logos* and what related to it, bringing to the fore a series of questions that later became the focus of the discipline of rhetoric. A more detailed analysis of problems of this sort should probably be undertaken by scholars of rhetoric. On this occasion, what I wish to emphasize is that we can only shed light on certain aspects if we focus on the importance of the theme of *logos* for the sophists. Only by doing so will we be able to reach a more adequate understanding of them.

Let us start from an initial misunderstanding. Usually, the attempt to confine the sophists to the field of rhetoric implies a contrast with philosophy (as in the case of Plato and Aristotle). In turn, the distinction

[42] The traditional reconstruction identified a first Sicilian stage, represented by two almost unknown figures, Tisias and Corax. From Sicily, rhetoric would then have reached Athens thanks to Gorgias (who famously visited Athens as an ambassador in 427 BC); in turn, Gorgias would have influenced other sophists such as Antiphon (assuming, of course, that the rhetor and the sophist of this name are one and the same person: see p. 128) and Thrasymachus. Among the modern champions of this view, see Kennedy 1963 and, more recently, Pernot 2006.

[43] See esp. Cole 1991: 71–112, and Gagarin 2007. Besides, the very adjective *rhetorike*, which has given us the term 'rhetoric', may have been coined by Plato: see Schiappa 1991: 40–9, along with the reservations voiced by Pernot 2006: 34–5.

between philosophy and rhetoric entails a contrast between different argumentative strategies: whereas philosophy is seen to uphold the ideal of rigorous reasoning, rhetoric is considered susceptible to the charm of a deceptive persuasion which appeals to people's feelings. But if we consider Gorgias' declamations or Antiphon's writings (particularly his *Tetralogies*, clusters of speeches each containing two speeches for the defence and two for the prosecution of a given case), we will soon realize that this is a false opposition. For, while it is true that the appeal to people's feelings plays an important role in the sophists' strategies, it is equally true that their efforts are largely focused on developing cogent and rigorous arguments.[44]

If we consider Gorgias and Antiphon, the two sophists about whom we have most information, several types of argument may be found in their texts: most notably, arguments from probability (or likelihood: *eikos*),[45] antinomy, induction from exemplary cases, *reductio ad absurdum*, and so-called *apagoge* (where the speaker explains all possibilities in order to then criticize each of them: this appears to be Gorgias' favourite strategy).[46] We may note that one of the major consequences of Gorgias' and Antiphon's interest in rhetoric is their considerable effort to identify and develop many different types of argument – the concrete object of the sophists' teaching.[47] The appeal to feelings is certainly important, but what is equally important is rational analysis. Ultimately, the reason for this interest is the need to carry out investigations in contexts where truth is not self-evident; and it would be

[44] See, for example, Lloyd 1979: 79–86.

[45] One variation of this argument is what we might call the 'counter-probability' argument: see e.g. Antiphon, *Tetral.* 1.2.2.3 and 2.2.6. A classic example is the case of a fight between a weak man and a strong one: in order to defend himself, the former argues that, being weak, it is unlikely that he wished to pick a fight with someone stronger. In turn, the latter replies by turning this reasoning on its head: it is unlikely that he was the one to start the fight because, being the stronger, he would immediately have been blamed for it. In other words, something is claimed to be unlikely precisely because it is likely: see Aristotle, *Rhetoric*, 2.24.12 (this argument was apparently 'invented' by Corax). The sophists' interest in the notion of 'probability' or 'likelihood', however, does not justify the criticism levelled by Plato, who in *Phaedrus*, 267a, accuses the sophists of choosing what is probable over what is true: for one only speaks of probability when the truth is unclear, which is often the case (unfortunately), but not always. See Gagarin 1994.

[46] The most complete analysis is provided by Spatharas 2001; see too Mazzara 1999 and Long 1984. On Antiphon, see the analysis by Gagarin 2007 (who quite rightly reacts to Solmsen 1931, according to whom all of Antiphon's orations were marked by the adoption of irrational argumentative schemes, such as the use of oaths and ordeals, which were typical of the archaic age). Thrasymachus was by contrast famous for his ability to play with the audience's feelings; see Macé 2008. For an overview, see also Tinsdale 2010.

[47] Natali 1986; see also above, Chapter 1, n. 11.

difficult to deny that this effort is irrelevant from a philosophical perspective.

This focus on argumentative strategies, moreover, makes it possible to rectify a second assumption, which seeks to reduce the sophists' teaching to a simple transmission of practical advice designed to ensure victory in an argument – as though achieving successful persuasion and winning contests were the only things that really mattered. No doubt, persuasion was crucial. But if we consider the surviving texts by Gorgias and the other sophists, we soon realize that it was not only a matter of persuading the listener: ultimately, it would be simplistic to think that the aim of declamations such as the *Encomium of Helen* or the *Defence of Palamedes* was simply to convince the audience of the innocence of two mythological figures.

Let us take, for instance, the aforementioned case of the *Encomium of Helen*, which Gorgias allegedly composed to defend the memory of Homer's celebrated heroine, guilty of fleeing with Paris and causing the Trojan War. To absolve Helen, Gorgias lists the four possible reasons that might have led her into Paris' arms, and shows that in all four cases she is not responsible: the responsibility would lie with the gods, or with Paris' force, or with the power of words, or with desire. Now, the attempt to cover all possibilities – this text is obviously based on the method of *apagoge* – clearly goes well beyond the need to persuade someone of Helen's innocence: to reach this objective, Gorgias only needed to stress traditional topics such as the will of the gods or Paris' physical force. Instead, he rather quickly moves beyond these topics, so as to focus on an analysis of the power of *logos* and *eros*. Indeed, while in this text Gorgias states his intention of persuading the public, his intention of eliciting pleasure is just as important. This is the pleasure derived from his display of intelligence, from his capacity to investigate the potential of language and human thought, and from his bold attempt to revisit – and at times criticize – traditional knowledge:

> If Gorgias were really trying to persuade his audience of Helen's innocence, he could have chosen a different strategy with a much greater chance of success.[48] But if his

[48] For example, he could have exploited an alternative version of the myth, according to which Helen never went to Troy (this is the version followed by the poet Stesichorus, among others: see Plato, *Phaedrus*, 243a–b; see too Herodotus 2.113–20 and Euripides' *Helen*). The argument that Helen was innocent, despite the fact that she went to Troy, instead betrays a desire to provoke the audience with a thesis that at first sight seems utterly implausible.

purpose was rather to enhance his reputation and demonstrate his intellectual virtuosity, then he may have felt that the more implausible the case appears initially, the more chance he has to show his skill in arguing for it as well as to develop novel perspective on the issues involved. . . .It does not matter whether anyone is persuaded of Helen's innocence; the important thing is that Gorgias' arguments open up new ways in which to think about language, emotion, causation, and responsibility. His case may be shocking, even perverse; it may be completely unconvincing; but his *logos* remains one of the most interesting and intellectually stimulating works of the sophistic period.[49]

Besides, all of this does not apply to Gorgias alone. For instance, a cursory reading of the *Dissoi logoi* is enough to show that the primary aim of its anonymous author is not simply to persuade his audience, for example when he notes that, in a race or war, victory is good for the winner but bad for the loser: the purpose of a claim of this sort is certainly not to persuade anyone that good and bad are the same thing. From Protagoras onwards, antilogy became the typical scheme of sophistic discussions, with opposing arguments being used as a means to examine a question in all of its complexity and ambiguity. When properly employed, this method could be of use for winning arguments; yet it was just as useful as a means to discuss problematic cases, investigate or develop different types of arguments, entertain the public or capture its interest, and showcase one's skills.[50] We here get to the very heart of the sophists' conceptualization: the analysis of *logos* served not just to develop rigorous and cogent arguments, but also to investigate various other aspects of human experience.[51]

This helps to clear up a third misunderstanding. The sophists have often been accused of being somewhat incoherent and unsystematic. Now, if no philosophy can exist without a system – that is, without a systematic and organized exposition of all the problems under scrutiny – it is legitimate to claim that there is no room for the sophists in this field. But such a rigid conception hardly does any justice to the richness of philosophy, which also includes enquiry and critical analysis as constitutive elements. According to this second, and more reasonable, definition, the sophists, too, have a place in philosophy, since, in order for it to truly work, the analysis of *logos* cannot be reduced to an investigation of argumentative techniques, but must also take into

[49] Gagarin 2001: 285–6.
[50] Gagarin 2001: 289.
[51] See Solmsen 1975.

consideration human reality and things in all their complexity. So it is easy to realize that the development of rhetoric promotes a deeper familiarity with human psychology and its underlying mechanisms.

Let us again consider the example of the *Encomium of Helen*. To better understand the phenomenon of communication, Gorgias investigates human physiology, emotional dynamics, and the power of mechanisms of persuasion: his analyses de facto imply a 'quasi-physical' conception of the soul, on which discourses exert a clear impact, eliciting concrete reactions.[52] In turn, this conception of the soul has very provocative consequences when it comes to human responsibility, or rather the lack thereof. For, if this is how the human soul works, then, no matter from what perspective we approach the problem, the conclusion will always be that Helen is innocent. But, clearly, Helen is not the problem here, since what is true in her case also applies to all human actions. So if Helen is innocent, no person is guilty of his or her actions.[53]

This is obviously a provocative thesis, and it may well be that not even Gorgias himself accepted it. Yet, through his arguments, Gorgias has the merit of having raised thorny problems that call for a more in-depth reflection on the concept (and existence) of responsibility and the idea of the subject that it assumes. Can an action performed under the impulse of a desire be considered a truly responsible action? And what about an action performed because of some external constraint? Thus far, the answer seems quite straightforward. But to what extent is Helen responsible with respect to the war that followed her flight? In a way, it was she who triggered it; but can she really be held accountable for it? And if so, is she also guilty? The problem becomes more complicated, and it is no coincidence that Protagoras and Antiphon had dealt with similar questions, by asking themselves who is really responsible for the death of a boy struck by a javelin (see p. 47 above). On the other hand, we might note that the question is not only interesting in itself, but is also so more generally in relation

[52] Segal 1962; Long 2015: 97–103. Along with *logos* and *eros*, another phenomenon to which Gorgias pays particular attention both in the *Encomium of Helen* and elsewhere (cf. 82B4 D.-K. =32D45a L.-M.) is sight. This has an intermediate function, so to speak, insofar as it transmits purely physical stimuli to the soul, engendering emotional states such as fear and joy, which in turn elicit certain behaviours according to the sequence: physical stimulus – emotional response – physical stimulus. In addition to the crucial study of Segal 1962: 105–7, see Casertano 1986 and Ioli 2010: 56–60, exploring a possible 'sophistic theory of perception'.

[53] See Barnes 1979: ii.524–30; Tordesillas 2008.

to human freedom, which now seems to have been obliterated by the force of human passions and the power of chance. Generally speaking, the sophists are not concerned with developing an exhaustive philosophical system: it is difficult to determine what the position of someone like Protagoras may have been with regard to the problem of determinism; and it is probably impossible to reconstruct a theory of moral responsibility for Gorgias. Yet this does not mean that the problems which their reflections raise in each case are unimportant. And it is precisely in this capacity to make crucial problems the centre focus of the debate, bringing out many previously undetected tensions, that the philosophical interest of the sophists lies.

Now that we have cleared up all these misunderstandings, having confirmed the importance of *logos* and the rationalist assumptions underlying the sophists' commitment to rhetoric, we can return to the problem of the philosophical significance of sophistic thought. The link between rhetoric and philosophy might seem paradoxical at first, given that traditionally – from Plato onwards – philosophy has developed in opposition to rhetoric: the claim that it is necessary to focus on rhetoric in order to understand the philosophical significance of sophistic thought might seem like utter nonsense. Yet it is actually true: the sophists' interest in *logos* and rhetoric does not lead them outside philosophy, but towards a different conception of philosophy. Their unsystematic approach, intellectual curiosity, and ambiguousness towards the problem of truth are all based on the insight we discussed in the previous chapter: the acknowledgement of the problematic nature of the reality that surrounds us and the awareness of the fact that *logos* is our only means to develop a relationship with reality.

Let us take the exemplary case of Gorgias once more. The celebration of *logos* that we find in the *Encomium* complements the thesis regarding the rift between thought and language put forward in the treatise *On Not-Being*. At first sight, this might seem problematic, and one might object that the treatise *On Not-Being* and the *Encomium of Helen* present mutually incompatible theses: whereas the former ends with an acknowledgement of the failure of words, the latter assigns the word a sort of divine omnipotence. Upon closer scrutiny, however, it is possible to reconcile these two positions, if we accept, on the one hand, that *On Not-Being* criticizes a certain conception of *logos*, and not *logos* as such; and, on the other, that the two declamations pick up from where the treatise had left off, so as to explore alternative possibilities. In this respect, the two declamations may be seen to constitute the constructive side, so to speak, of a two-part work which also comprised the deconstructionist treatise *On Not-Being*.[54]

The discussion on *logos* is therefore essential for assessing the distance which separates Gorgias and the other sophists from the traditional conception of philosophy, the Parmenidean conception, which was partly taken up by Plato and Aristotle. The sophists' polemical target is the claim to establish *logos* as a foundation, based on the assumption that being, thought, and reality coincide, whereby *logos* is thought to express truth in the sense of a true and objective representation of reality. But this is impossible, according to the sophists: reality is intrinsically multifarious and resists any unitary reconstruction; and because human *logos* is always subjective or relative, it always represents a given point of view or opinion, and not absolute truth. This is where the sophists' alternative conception comes into play: they assign *logos* the function not of stating the truth, but of giving meaning to reality, of turning multiplicity into some kind of order – a provisional order, yet one still capable of orienting human actions. To paraphrase Nietzsche (who appreciated the sophists precisely because of such theses), it is a matter of interpreting things, since there are no facts, but only interpretations. Alternatively, and more radically, it is possible to draw a distinction between ontology and logology:

> Ontology: discourse celebrates being, its function is to speak it. Logology: discourse makes being, being is an effect of speaking. In the former case, the exterior imposes itself, and requires that we speak it; in the latter case, discourse produces the exterior.[55]

Logos can prove successful because – as we have seen – despite its apparent inconsistency, it is actually very powerful. Paradoxically, Gorgias' emphasis on the limits of human experience ultimately leads to a celebration of the capacity of *logos* to give meaning to everything.

From *logos* to *nomos*, from language to politics

As repeatedly noted over the course of this chapter, the sophists can truly make a claim to being specialists of *logos*. Clearly, this is such an important term that it can hardly be made the exclusive preserve

[54] Ioli 2010: 90. On the function of language in Gorgias, see also Calogero 1932: 262 and esp. Mourelatos 1985: 627–30.

[55] Cassin 1995: 73.

of the sophists: the concept of *logos*, with all that it entails, was just as important for the Presocratics, as well as for Plato, Aristotle, and all other Greek philosophers. Still, the sophists' contribution here remains crucial. It was thanks to them that an awareness of the fact that *logos* is the distinctive feature of humankind emerged. Whereas for many previous thinkers, *logos* is what enables us to get in touch with an objective and well-ordered reality, since *logos* is also the ordering principle of reality, for the sophists it is a tool that a human can – and must – use to give meaning to things, a meaning that things do not necessarily possess in themselves. The problem, in other words, is to build a relationship with an ever-elusive reality and to adapt to changing situations, finding the right measure in each case. Thus the problem of *logos* is the problem of *kairos*, the right moment: the problem of finding the best possible solution in each circumstance and of knowing how to express it.[56]

In themselves, when viewed in abstract terms, however, *logos* and *kairos* are not enough to describe the sophists' position. The attempt to give meaning to reality cannot be confined to the theoretical level of words, but must concretely manifest itself in the shaping of a human world: in order to possess any real value, the sophists' *logos* must engage with the ambiguous world of politics, where nothing is fixed and duplicity is the norm. It is hardly a coincidence that the first people to be referred to as sophists were politicians such as Mnesiphilus, who had helped Themistocles:

> Who was neither an orator nor one of the so-called 'natural philosophers', but who, practicing something that at that time was called 'wisdom' (*sophia*) but was really cleverness in political matters and pragmatic shrewdness, made this his profession and preserved it intact like a sect transmitted to him in succession from Solon. But those people who followed him mixed this with forensic arts and transferred its sphere of

[56] Scholars have long been debating the importance of the notion of *kairos* for the sophists – a notion that was widespread in the archaic Greek world. The problem is twofold: first, to determine whether the sophists developed a rhetorical theory of *kairos* (thereby acknowledging the importance of improvisation); and second, to determine whether they also assigned *kairos* a more general value, which might make it the notion that best expresses the specific nature of sophistic knowledge. The few surviving sources allow us to give a positive answer to the first problem (in 82B13 D.K. = 32D12 L.-M., Gorgias is even credited with a *kairou techne*; cf. 82A1a, A24 and B13 D.-K. [= 32D11–12 L.-M.]; 80A1 D.-K. [= 31D20DL.-M.] on Protagoras and Alcidamas' speech *On Those Who Write Written Speeches, or On the Sophists*). As regards the second problem, the existence of a general doctrine of *kairos* (a '*Kairos*-Lehre', to quote Guthrie 1971: 272 n. 4) seems like a projection on the part of modern scholars – a fascinating, yet at least partly anachronistic, view; see Tortora 1985 and Tordesillas 1986.

application from action to speeches, and they were called 'sophists'.

(Plutarch, *Life of Themistocles*, 2 = Soph. R4 L.-M)[57]

As is well known – and as one would expect in the historical and cultural context of the fifth century – the sophists extensively dealt with practical and political matters. It is important to note that this was not a self-contained interest, but the direct consequence of their enquiries into *physis* and *logos*:

> to put it in even more provocative terms, the blueprint for the sophists' politics is provided by the treatise *On Not-Being*. . . .Ultimately, being is but a consequence of saying. Given this, it is clear that the presence of Being, the immediacy of Nature, and the evidence of a speech designed to adequately express these things, all vanish together: the natural philosopher who discovers speech gives way to the politician who creates discourse.[58]

The emphasis on the creative power of speech enables the sophist to take the place of the philosopher who expresses being and of the poet who claims to be the spokesman for divine truth; and this is precisely how he comes to affirm his leading position in the world of the *polis*. Along with *physis* and *logos*, a third concept is of crucial importance in order to understand the sophists, specifically *nomos*, and it is this concept that we must now focus on.

[57] See also Detienne 2006: 205.
[58] Cassin 1995: 152.

IV JUSTICE AND LAW

The fifth century is the century of *nomos*, a concept difficult to translate, as it covers several different semantic fields. Usually *nomos* is rendered as 'law', but this is a reductive translation, since the term describes not just positive laws but also traditions, customs, and established practices. Besides, as Aristotle was to observe, the two meanings 'law' and 'tradition' are closely related: 'For the law has no power to command obedience except that of habit, which can only be given by time' (*Politics*, 1269a20). In short, *nomos* is anything which is assigned some value, any norm accepted by a group. From the late sixth century onwards, this term acquired a central place in the Greek world, becoming a privileged object of reflection for the sophists. The most significant element is its spread as a technical term for written law, particularly in Athenian democracy.[1] Prior to this, it chiefly referred to customs and traditions. Yet its growing importance is not devoid of problematic aspects. The greater economic and political stability attained through the victorious wars against the Persians led to an increase in travel, cultural exchanges, and trade, which contributed to broadening the perspectives and knowledge of the Greeks. One of the most striking observations they made concerned the wide range of laws and traditions in force in the various cities and states: *nomos* is indeed a crucial value, as the law and tradition governing the life of a community; but it is in any case relative, as it varies from city to city. The acknowledgement of the relativity of *nomos* is a central theme in fifth-century literature, as may be inferred from some famous passages by Pindar, Herodotus, and Aeschylus.[2] At first sight, the conclusions reached by these authors would appear to emphasize the capacity of *nomos* to impose itself: as a verse by Pindar states, *nomos* 'is the king of all things' (fr. 169a Snell-Mähler). Yet the ascertainment of the range of laws and traditions in existence could also lead to moral relativism and to the conclusion that there are no absolute, universal or objective values (*Dissoi logoi*, 90, 2.18 D.-K. = 40, 2.18 L.-M.).

Confronted with the problem of *nomos*, the sophists were divided: some upheld its importance, while others sharply criticized its weakness. In order to better articulate their polemic, the latter could also

[1] Ostwald 1969.
[2] De Romilly 2005: 49–66.

rely on another key concept in Greek philosophical reflection, namely *physis*, a term which is usually translated as 'nature', although a more fitting translation for it would probably be 'reality', at least with reference to these debates. As already noted in Chapter 2, *physis* was an important term for the reflection of naturalist thinkers, from Thales to Anaxagoras, from Empedocles to Democritus: it stands for the nature of things. In the fifth century, chiefly through the contribution of medical knowledge, *physis* mostly came to be used to refer to human nature. In all cases, whether it was used to refer to humans or to all things, the term described the stable, invariable character of things or human beings. The relation between *nomos* and *physis* is probably the topic most fiercely debated by fifth-century authors:[3] it offers a conceptual scheme that can fruitfully be applied to a wide range of subjects, such as the legitimacy of slavery, the equality or inequality of human beings, and the existence of the gods (is the inequality of humans or the existence of the gods a natural fact or a cultural product?). Yet it is especially in relation to the theme of justice and the law that the sophists exploited this pair of terms in the most original way.[4]

Justice according to Protagoras

The first author to have extensively discussed justice was probably Protagoras: indeed, according to the Peripatetic Aristoxenus, 'the *Republic*...was almost entirely written in Protagoras' *Antilogies*' (80B5 D.-K. = 31R1a L.-M.). Aristoxenus is often malicious towards Plato, and his accusation of plagiarism is no doubt excessive. The fact remains that Plato was very interested in Protagoras' reflections on political problems, acknowledging their relation to ontological and epistemological theses: the aforementioned evidence from the *Theaetetus* and *Protagoras* suggests that the discussion of justice and *nomos* stemmed directly from the thesis of relativism.[5] Therefore, in order to grasp the meaning of Protagoras' analyses of justice and law, it is necessary to briefly return to the points made in Chapter 2. In the *Theaetetus*, one of the most significant consequences of the 'man-measure' thesis is the validity and legitimacy of all opinions and judgements. In the *Protagoras*, this

[3] Heinimann 1945.
[4] Hoffmann 1997.
[5] See now Gavray 2017.

coincides with relativity and plurality of interests and use (80A22 D.-K., not in L.-M.). There are no absolute and objective values, such as truth and goodness, to guide the judgements and choices of humans (and similar considerations also apply to the issue of the gods, regarding which Protagoras stood out for his agnostic position: see Chapter 6). All these claims present some interesting theoretical perspectives, but also some serious practical problems: in the absence of any objective values or norms, the risk is that of a potential conflict of everyone against everyone else, whereby each person will pursue their own interest on the basis of what they consider to be good for them. But while this is certainly a possibility, it is not the only one. Protagoras believes that, unlike animals, human beings can reach an agreement, thereby neutralizing these destructive drives. To promote this agreement is the duty of the sophist, of the true politician, and of any good citizen: it is a matter of laying down some communal rules and values, so as to safeguard everyone's interests by promoting mutual collaboration.

This is what can be inferred from the relativism of the 'man-measure' thesis, which has significant practical consequences and lays the foundations for the Protagorean conception of justice. In the so-called 'Apology of Protagoras' in the *Theaetetus*, the sophist – who is explaining the correct meaning of the 'man-measure' thesis to Socrates – states that 'whatever seems [or: is decreed to be, *dokein*] just and fine to each city also *is* that for it, so long as it thinks [or: adopts this law, *nomizein*]' (80A21a D.-K. = 31D38 L.-M.). Consistently with what has been noted so far, justice, not unlike truth or goodness, is not an objective, absolute, or divine value, but the result of human decisions – a set of rules that humans establish together. In practice, justice consists in *nomos*, understood both as a body of written laws (the law code) and as a range of values and traditions (the moral code) on which a community is founded.

From a more strictly juridical perspective, with reference to written law, we can argue that Protagoras offers the earliest attestation of what was later to be described as 'legal positivism', which is to say the thesis that law and justice coincide: the just is what is established by law.[6] In order to provide a complete overview of Protagoras' theory, however, we must take account of a third element, which is to say what is useful. In the absence of any absolute good, what provides the

[6] Neschke-Hentske 1995: 56–9.

foundations for – and lends legitimacy to – the law (and hence justice) is precisely the concept of what is advantageous and useful for the parties who are striking an agreement. Naturally, in this case too we cannot think of what is useful as an objective good: as people's interests vary depending on the situation, it is not something which one must conform to, but rather something to be constructed out of different points of view. It is precisely this capacity to promote an agreement based on what is useful that reveals the importance of the sophist or his pupil, the politician.[7] Their duty is to help the city establish rules and values, which will then take the concrete form of a body of laws (*nomoi*) allowing the city to prosper: 'the clever and competent orators [i.e. those who publicly discuss political matters, hence politicians and sophists] make good things seem to be just to cities instead of bad ones' (A21a D.-K. = 31D38 L.-M.).[8]

Similar conclusions are suggested by an analysis of the famous myth that Plato puts into Protagoras' mouth in the other dialogue devoted to the sophist, the *Protagoras* (80C1 D.-K. = 31D40 L.-M.). Some scholars have questioned the reliability of this testimony, arguing that it is due more to Plato's genius than Protagoras' pen. No doubt, this is a reasonable observation, because it would be too much to assume that Plato simply incorporated a long extract from an opponent's work into his own text. Yet the reasonableness of this observation does not justify the opposite – and equally radical – hypothesis that the myth is simply Plato's own invention and has nothing to do with Protagoras. This assumption, too, conflicts with Plato's way of working, since – as we have seen in relation to the 'man-measure' thesis, for instance – Plato always sets out from his opponents' theses in order to criticize them. The myth (like the speech that follows it) certainly offers some information on Protagoras' thought; to what extent, it is difficult to determine.[9]

The myth retraces the key stages in the history of humankind, starting from the well-known story of Prometheus, the beneficent daemon. When the time had come to generate mortal animals (including humans), the gods entrusted Prometheus with assigning each species

[7] See also Denyer 2013: 167.

[8] It is worth noting once more that, obviously, the laws will apply 'so long as the city thinks [or: adopts this law, *nomizein*]': as a human product, no law can claim to have absolute and everlasting validity.

[9] For an analysis of these problems, see Bonazzi 2011 and Manuwald 2013.

qualities that would allow it to survive and prosper. Prometheus (literally, 'he who understands first, who foresees') left the task up to his brother Epimetheus ('he who understands afterwards'), but the latter forgot humans: 'while he was in perplexity, Prometheus came to check the distribution, and he saw that the other animals were suitably provided with everything, but that man was naked, unshod, uncovered, and unarmed' (*Prot.* 321c4–7). To make up for his brother's mistake, Prometheus stole fire and technical expertise from the gods, allowing humans to approach the world of the gods, learn how to speak, and master the technologies required to solve practical life problems – the provision of food, clothing, and housing. However, despite this progress, humanity risked becoming extinct, as it lacked political wisdom ('for that was in Zeus' possession' [*Prot.* 321d5–6], in a realm to which Prometheus – who was being punished for the theft – no longer had access): only this wisdom would allow humans to organize themselves into social groups and live together, so as to protect themselves from wild animals and natural dangers. Humans were trying to save themselves by coming together in cities, but 'when they gathered together, they committed injustice against one another...so that they scattered once again and were destroyed' (*Prot.* 322b7–8). Finally, fearing that the human race would meet extinction, Zeus despatched Hermes to distribute justice (*dike*) and shame (*aidos*), not in the same way as with the other forms of arts (whereby, for instance, one physician is enough for many patients), but to everyone indiscriminately: 'for cities would not exist if only a few men have a share in these things [shame and justice], as in other arts' (*Prot.* 323c8–d2). Such is Zeus's law (*nomos*).

The myth (and the long speech that follows it) helps clarify the anthropological ideas that lie at the basis of the Protagorean conception of *nomos* and justice. Even though it is articulated in three phases, the myth must not be understood in a chronological sense, as though it retraced the various stages in human civilization; rather, Protagoras' account is meant to identify and circumscribe some essential features of humankind itself: what we have is not a 'genetic' myth but a 'structural' one.[10] The state of nature in which humans find themselves living after their creation reflects an impossible situation, and may be understood as a counter-factual example to demonstrate *e contrario* that

[10] For an in-depth investigation of these topics and further bibliographical references, see Farrar 1988: 81–99; Bonazzi 2004; Balla 2018: 91–101.

human beings are political and rational animals: they are political in the sense that they cannot live in isolation, but need one another and are forced to live together ('political' is to be understood etymologically starting from the *polis* – the city, community, and state); and they are rational because they have the means to engage with one another in order to find possible solutions.

As we have seen, these solutions are only possible through the sharing of collective values: in the myth, justice and shame are not a permanent possession of humankind, but rather predispositions that must be actualized, which is to say that they must take the concrete form of *nomos*, to ensure the development of a harmonious community.[11] In order to clarify Protagoras' position, it is worth referring again to the conceptual pair *nomos/physis*: for Protagoras, human *physis*, unlike that of other animals, is not a given or something invariable; rather, it can only be fully realized through *nomos*, which actualizes the specific potential of humanity – a political potential.[12] Whereas animals will always behave in the same way, humans can decide how to comport themselves: whether to plunge back into the violence of the animal world or to fashion a world of values for themselves. *Nomos* – which is to say, the development of a political society – does not stand in contrast to *physis*, but rather constitutes its 'fulfilment'[13] and ensures the existence of individuals. Moreover, *nomos* is not only what ensures survival, but also – and most importantly – the precondition for humans to fully express their potential. The individual – every individual human being – is the product of society and attains fulfilment in society: hence, his or her ultimate fulfilment depends on the existence of a well-ordered society.

Again, this explains the social function of the sophist, a master of political virtue: the sophist, just like the politician and any good citizen, exercises a fundamental function for the community, insofar as he promotes this collective awareness, thereby contributing to perfecting his community, which can and must be improved.[14] In other words, it is

[11] Moreover, we should not overlook the fact that, while Zeus is the one who bestows these two virtues on humanity, he does not concretely define what comprises them by making their content explicit: in other words, justice is not a divine revelation, but something that humans must achieve together. In this sense, the mythological framework does not conflict with the agnosticism of fragment 80B4 D.-K. (= 31D10 L.-M.).

[12] Later in the dialogue, Protagoras speaks of political virtue as human virtue (*andros arete*) *tout court* (*Prot.* 325a); on this issue see also Beresford 2013.

[13] Casertano 1971: 124.

[14] Decleva Caizzi 1999: 319.

necessary to promote a critical reflection on the community's choices. In its ideal representation, the city emerges as a permanent educational apparatus,[15] while the law, *nomos*, ultimately coincides with what is useful for the individual and the community: respecting and favouring the *nomoi* benefits everyone because it safeguards the community. The theory developed by Protagoras thus seems capable of answering one of the main problems in political philosophy, that of obligation, of why it is necessary to obey the law.

Protagoras' theses concerning justice and humankind certainly represent some of the greatest achievements of the sophists, the importance of which emerges even more clearly when examined within the broader context of the Greek tradition. The belief that *nomos* is what distinguishes humans from animals, insofar as it allows them to transcend the world of brute force and violence by creating an order based on shared values, is not a new idea that Protagoras introduced. The very same thesis is also found in Hesiod, who – along with Homer – was the great educator-poet of the Greek world:[16]

> Perses, lay these things in your heart
> And give heed to Justice, and put violence entirely out of your mind.
> This is the law (*nomos*) that Cronus' son has established for human beings:
> That fish and beasts and winged birds
> eat one another, since Justice is not among them;
> but to human beings he has given Justice, which is the best by far.
> (Hesiod, *Works and Days*, 274–80)

The thesis found in Hesiod is essentially the same as the one later adopted by Protagoras, and the reference to this text is intended precisely to emphasize such a convergence: what is typical of human beings, and what distinguishes them from animals, is their possession of justice, which is to say their political capacity. Plato's Protagoras makes a brilliant attempt to reclaim the tradition, by highlighting the continuity between his own theses and its precepts.[17] However, this attempt does not amount to an uncritical borrowing, because Protagoras' appropriation is also a deformation, and the differences with respect to Hesiod are no less significant than the similarities. According to Hesiod, Justice is divine: it is a deity, the daughter and

[15] Pl. *Prot.* 325c5–326e5. See also Vegetti 1989: 51.
[16] See Bonazzi 2011.
[17] Sihvola 1989: 39–48.

protégée of Zeus, who intervenes when he sees that men fail to respect her (*Works and Days*, 257, 265; *Theogony*, 901–3). All mythological imagery aside, this means that justice exists regardless of human beings; human justice is not independent of this order of divine values, but must rather conform to it. The situation radically changes with Protagoras: the innovation consists in his emphasis on the human rather than the divine, and the relative, rather than absolute, character of justice.[18] There is no place for divinity: justice is something human – it is not what brings us close to the gods but what fulfils our natural potential. Protagoras', then, is a radical humanism; and it is in the light of this humanism that the way in which he modifies Hesiod's position becomes clear. Whereas in Hesiod the present age (the Age of Iron) is characterized precisely by the flight of Justice and Shame (*Works and Days*, 190–201), in Protagoras the association of the human community, *polis*, and justice also suggests that some form of justice and shame is always to be found – as long as there are human beings. In turn, this strengthens the reasonable belief that acting in view of justice is in everyone's interests. Whereas Hesiod defines human history in terms of decadence (since it is difficult to imitate the gods), Protagoras presents it as the history of a possible progress.

The engagement with Hesiod, which constitutes the real subtext of the myth, confirms the underlying aim of Plato's presentation: to highlight the great ambition of Protagoras, who had not so much sought to engage in erudite debate with other wise men, as to present himself as an heir to the Greek *paideia*, as one of the great masters or, rather, as *the* great master of Greek culture, capable of imparting a teaching that drew upon tradition but that could also meet the needs of the new times (consider the observations already made on pp. 51–52).

That this was Protagoras' aim becomes even clearer when we consider another of the great topics discussed in fifth-century Athens: democracy. Generally speaking, Protagorean humanism was well suited to Athenian democracy, so much so that it has been argued that his theses

[18] In all likelihood, another implicit polemical aim of Protagoras' thesis is to be found in those 'unwritten and unfailing ordinances (*nomima*) of the gods, which have life, not simply today and yesterday, but for ever' (Sophocles, *Antigone*, 453–5) – on which see e.g. De Romilly 2005: 27–48. Nor can it be ruled out that, in emphasizing the importance of these unwritten laws, fifth-century authors such as Sophocles were precisely targeting positivists such as Protagoras and Pericles: see Bonazzi 2017: 112–24, in the footsteps of Ehrenberg 1957.

provide 'a theoretical basis for participatory democracy'.[19] With its rejection of alleged absolute truths in favour of the vindication of the legitimacy of opinions, the 'man-measure' thesis – when applied to the political field – clearly serves to defend one of the cornerstones of Athenian democracy, *isegoria*, namely every citizen's right to express his ideas in the assembly. Without having to posit that Protagoras' doctrines were developed precisely for this purpose, it is possible to note that they offered some insights that were far from irrelevant to the new political phase that Athens was experiencing.

Even more significant are the implications that can be drawn from the myth of Prometheus and Epimetheus. The defence of the political dimension of human nature helps bring out the distinctiveness of the democratic system compared to other political systems: if the human being is a political animal who only achieves fulfilment in a political context, it is clear that democracy, as the government in which all citizens are allowed to take part, is the system that allows all humans to fulfil their nature (and to concretely bring attention to their needs). In other words, insofar as it fulfils this requirement, democracy represents not one form of government among others – albeit a better one – but rather the form of government par excellence, the only truly 'human' one: the government of all. This idea of democracy as government of all, as the government of the people as a whole and not just of a part of it, which is to say the popular faction (to use the Latin terminology: as the government of the *populus* rather than the *plebs*), was repeatedly exploited by Athenian democratic propaganda.[20] This emphasis on the community, moreover, is used to justify another cornerstone of democracy, arguably the most important one, namely the very close bond that

[19] Kerferd 1981a: 144. A particularly important study on this topic is Farrar 1988. In order to better evaluate Protagoras' thesis – and, more generally, those of Athenian democracy – we must distinguish between the theoretical level and that of concrete praxis. The reason for this is that Athenian democracy has often been accused of being anything but a 'democracy', given that roughly three-quarters of the population (women, slaves, and foreigners resident in Attica) were barred from political participation. These are undeniable historical facts. Yet in no way do they weaken the interest of theories such as those of Protagoras or Pericles, who promote an important elaboration of the concept of democracy, understood as the government of the community. Ideas of this sort still preserve all their importance today, regardless of the inconsistent way in which they were applied in fifth-century Athens.

[20] What proves crucial in this respect is the testimony of Thucydides, who, when discussing the democratic ideology, repeatedly adopts the same perspective as Protagoras. The most clear-cut stance is expressed in Athenagoras' speech in Book 6: 'democracy (*demos*) is the name for all, oligarchy for only a part' (Thuc. 6.39). No less important is Pericles' famous funerary speech for the fallen of the first year of war, in which democracy is described as the government not of 'the few' but of 'the many' for 'everyone' (on this climax, see Musti 1995: 3–13).

must hold together the city's interest and the individual's, where the former is the precondition for the latter.[21] Protagoras, in other words, emerges as a democratic political thinker: he is a political thinker because he has shown that the social (or political – from *polis*) dimension is fundamental; he is democratic insofar as he suggests that political action is a collective and shared kind of action.

The new democratic political order is not imposed from above, but is immanent and structured on two levels – those of competency and excellence. As citizens, all people have a basic political competence, which some people know how to make use of more than others (the sophist here marks out a special area in which he can apply his expertise); but all this invariably takes place through a mutual engagement.[22] Presenting democracy, the form of government for the new times, as the heir and culmination of the Greek political tradition, is certainly a brilliant achievement, which legitimizes Protagoras' aspirations and ambitions. It is hardly a coincidence that the main ancient reflections on democracy were often set in relation to Protagoras' ideas.[23]

In Protagoras, therefore, we find a first, vigorous defence of *nomos*, an idea of which the fifth-century Greeks were particularly proud. Protagoras was not completely isolated, as other authors and texts associated with sophistry appear to have shared his positive evaluation of law. The text closest to Protagoras' views is arguably the so-called Anonymous of Iamblichus, an anonymous treatise quoted at length in the Neoplatonist Iamblichus' *Protrepticus*. No less interesting are some extracts from an oration, *Against Aristogeiton*, falsely attributed to Demosthenes but more likely dating from the late fifth century. Its author once again emphasizes the thesis that law and justice are what allow humans to distinguish themselves from animals, by transcending the world of violence: nature is disorderly and a source of injustice, whereas the law ensures what is right, good, and beneficial (anon. *On the Laws*, 15–20). Finally, Aristotle credits Lycophron with a 'protectionist' conception of law ('law is…the guarantor for each other of

[21] For some interesting parallels, see Thuc. 2.40.2 and 2.60.2–4 (Pericles' speech), and Hdt. 5.78.

[22] Farrar 1988: 81–7.

[23] In particular, in addition to the aforementioned passages by Thucydides, it is worth mentioning the famous comparison between the various forms of government found in Herodotus 3.80–2. Finally, it is worth recalling that the seventh section of the *Dissoi logoi* also discussed democracy and how best to safeguard it.

what is just', 83.3 D.-K. = 38D3 L.-M.), which can probably be understood as one of the first attestations of contractualist theories (of which there is a compelling formulation in Glaucon's speech at the beginning of the second book of Plato's *Republic*): the idea that laws guarantee rights evidently implies a 'disorderly' conception of human nature. Laws are designed to protect people, which is why they must be respected: at least in this sense, the 'protectionist' and the contractualist theories converge.[24]

Unfortunately, the dearth of information about these authors makes it impossible to reconstruct in any detail the relation between them and Protagoras, whose theses certainly attracted much attention in Athens and Greece; but it is not unreasonable to hypothesize that they drew upon his work in some way. Besides, the fact that Protagoras constituted an important point of reference in the debates on such matters may also be inferred from the theses of sophists opposed to *nomos*, whose arguments – as we shall now see – appear to have had precisely the thinker of Abdera as their target.

Against *nomos*: from Gorgias to Callicles

The other great sophist, Gorgias, does not appear to have devoted any special attention to justice and other political issues. Here it is possible to register a substantial difference compared to Protagoras: whereas the latter attributed the utmost importance to the teaching of political virtue, the former apparently even went so far as to claim that he did not teach virtue at all:

> What I admire most of all in Gorgias, Socrates, is that you would never hear him promise this [*sc.* to be a teacher of virtue]. Instead he laughs at other people when he hears them make this promise. No, he thinks that one should make people clever at speaking.
> (82A21 D.-K. = 32D47 L.-M.)

Contrary to what might seem to be the case, however, the opposition between the two does not lie so much in that between the centrality of politics on the one hand and the lack of political involvement on the other: rhetoric, the object of Gorgias' teaching, is the political art par excellence, which teaches one how to persuade a crowd or

[24] More generally, on the possible circulation of contractualist theories in the fifth century, see Guthrie 1971: 135–47 and Kahn 1981.

manipulate its decisions; it is the art that ensures domination (82A27 D.-K. = 32D7a–b L.-M.). Therefore, as Plato had realized in the *Gorgias*, even Gorgias' teaching is political, in its own way. The true difference lies in Gorgias' greater degree of conformism compared to Protagoras, who had sought to establish a critical relation to traditional values, rejecting some values while adopting others. Gorgias instead seems to have no interest in critically engaging with traditional beliefs, which he readily accepts (see, for example, 82B18–19 D.-K. = 32D53 L.-M.). What matters is not to call a given value system into question, but rather to find self-affirmation within such a system: this is the aim of rhetoric, and the success that it ensures is what Gorgias is concerned with.

In other words, it could be argued that Protagoras attempts to reconcile the society's reasons with those of individuals, whereas Gorgias focuses on the interests of the individual in contrast to life in society. The evidence we have does not allow us to claim that, for Gorgias, the defence of individuals also entails an openly hostile stance towards society, as was later the case with other sophists. But this contrast is at least theoretically possible, and explains why Gorgias too can be included – if only in a nuanced way – among those sophists who were critical of *nomos*, understood as the law governing the relations between citizens within a community.

Significant confirmation of this is provided by the fragment of an epitaph written to commemorate the fallen Athenians (82B5a–b and 6 D.-K. = 32D29, 30a–b, 28 L.-M.). This speech, a fine example of Gorgias' prose, is entirely played out in oppositions and contrasts, which are used to celebrate the qualities of the dead soldiers. Unsurprisingly, these qualities coincide with traditional values, such as respect for one's parents and veneration of the gods. Yet this traditionalism heightens the choice to list justice (*dikaion*) and law (*nomos*) among the negative terms: 'often preferring gentle equity to implacable justice, and often the correctness of words to the punctiliousness of law'. This is certainly a bold expression, which explains why, shortly afterwards, Gorgias makes an allusion to the 'most divine and most universal law' ('considering the most divine and most universal law to be this: both to say and to leave unsaid, and to do < and to leave undone > what is necessary when it is necessary'). However, it is evident that this religious veneer is only used to introduce a recurrent theme in Gorgias' thought, namely the importance of the opportune moment (*kairos*): the 'most divine law' is the capacity to say and do opportune things at the opportune moment. And this is precisely what justice and law lack, insofar as they purport to control and dominate the complex and elusive reality of human experience. The rigidity of the law is thus set in contrast to the flexibility of intelligence, which is capable of adapting its reasoning to the existing circumstances, so as to favour the best and hence most 'correct' situations.[25] This contrast between intelligence and law betrays a degree of impatience with *nomos* and was repeatedly taken up by many thinkers, as we shall see later on in this chapter and in the following one, to the point that it came to be regarded as a distinguishing feature of the sophists (see Thucydides 3.37).

A second interesting insight is provided by the *Encomium of Helen*: among the various reasons adduced in Helen's defence, we find power. If Helen has followed Paris as a result of the will of a superior being, the goddess Aphrodite, it is not right to blame Helen:

> For by nature the stronger is not prevented by the weaker, but the weaker is ruled and led by the stronger, and the stronger directs, the weaker follows. But a god is stronger than a human in force, in intelligence, and in all respects. So if the responsibility is to be ascribed to Fortune and to a god, Helen too is to be freed from ill repute.
> (82B11, 6 D.-K. = 32D24, 6 L.-M.)

In this case, too, the mythological scheme (the reference to the superiority of gods over humans – but let us not forget that ultimately the gods are equated with destiny) conceals a far from obvious idea, which de facto constitutes a first justification of strength as the criterion guiding human actions:

> the form still conforms to traditional patterns, but the principle is now used to justify the general law of the supremacy of the stronger, which, within the framework of the mythological example and scheme, is geared towards the acknowledgement of a truth that de facto operates in the world of human beings.[26]

Again, what we have here is an idea destined to prove highly influential in the future.

A radical redevelopment of the insights provided by Gorgias is offered by Callicles, a mysterious figure who is only known to us through Plato's *Gorgias*, where he is featured – significantly – as a friend, guest, and in a way pupil of Gorgias'. Given the silence of our

[25] Note the importance of this concept: see Chapter 3, p. 48.
[26] Isnardi Parente 1969: 172.

sources, some scholars have doubted his very existence. However, it is more likely that Callicles was an actual Athenian nobleman who died young in the years of the Peloponnesian War, leaving little memory of himself outside his circle of acquaintances (which included Plato: many of the characters associated with Callicles as his friends, lovers, or relatives may be traced back to Plato's own milieu). For Plato this young aristocrat embodied a certain way of thinking, an unscrupulous 'philosophy of life' deeply influenced by the sophists' theses (despite Callicles' professed contempt for the sophists: see *Gorgias*, 520a), a philosophy which must have enjoyed a considerable degree of popularity in Athens in the war years.[27]

At first sight, Callicles' thesis presents itself as an all-out attack against *nomos* and as a celebration of *physis*. In particular, it consists in the distinction between two different laws: law in accordance with nature and law against nature. Whereas nature shows that strength is the only criterion of value ('nature itself reveals that it's just thing for the better man and the more capable man to have a greater share than the worse man and the less capable man', *Gorgias*, 483c–d), in the human world it is the weak who dominate by forcing the strong and best to respect laws against nature, which proclaim false values such as equality and moderation (483b–c). Evidently, the polemical reference here is to democratic *nomos*, to which Callicles opposes – with an almost religious emphasis – nature's law, prophesying the triumph of the strongest and of true justice, namely justice in accordance with nature, which stems from strength and the ability to overpower others (483e–484a).

Callicles' statements are provocative not just because of their openly anti-democratic tone, but also – and especially – because of their implications. In support of his thesis that nature regulates itself through force, Callicles adduces the examples of what occurs in cities and families (alluding to imperialist wars of conquest and to the practice of slavery), and of the behaviour of animals. This juxtaposition is far from neutral, insofar as it entails a rejection of human specificity, which the Greek tradition from Hesiod to Protagoras had stressed: the idea of the long journey of human beings, who with much difficulty emerge from the violent animal world through *nomos*, is wholly rejected as a false and tendentious account, which distorts reality out of fear of the

[27] Dodds 1959: 12–15.

truth. The key word in Callicles' speech, his truth, is *pleonexia*, literally the drive 'to have more'; and it is this unsuppressible instinct to overpower others, this will and desire to increase one's own power, that is the hallmark of all things – of humans, of animals, and indeed of the whole universe (cf. *Gorgias*, 508a).

Callicles' claims are certainly intriguing, as is shown for instance by the fact that Friedrich Nietzsche drew upon them in some famous pages of his *Genealogy of Morals*.[28] However, it is easy to show that they are weak theses. The main difficulty lies in the conflating of the descriptive and prescriptive aspects of the concept of *nomos*, or law. To clarify the problem, we can consider the modern distinction of the term in the scientific field and in the legal one: scientific laws, which describe the behaviour of a given object (be it a lion or a planet), are one thing; the laws issued by legislators, which prescribe a certain type of action (such as the paying of taxes or the avoidance of murder), are another. In other words, to state how things are is different from stating how they should be.

Callicles' thesis ultimately boils down to an attempt to make these two aspects coincide, but it falls short of its mark. Like a scientist, he sets out from the descriptive aspect, yet, unlike the scientist, he also assigns it axiological value. Thus, it is an objective fact that reality regulates itself according to power relations, but this is not understood as something neutral, but rather as something good and just: to use Callicles' own words, there is a natural justice, and this is *pleonexia*, which is to say the law of the strongest. But herein lies the problem. The fact that reality axiologically regulates itself according to power relations means that the one who prevails is the strongest and hence the most just. But given that Callicles' world is dominated by those whom he contemptuously refers to as the mass of weaklings, it follows that the weak are actually the strong and hence the just: the democratic *nomos* of equality is therefore just and beautiful, whereas the 'strong' (that is, those regarded as strong and best by Callicles, the aristocrats) are de facto losers and weaklings.[29] In other words, establishing strength as the criterion of value implies an acceptance of reality, and not its rejection, which is what Callicles opts for when he calls for the overthrow of the tyranny of the weak. Significantly, later on in the dialogue,

[28] See Dodds 1959: 387–91.

[29] A similar reasoning, intended to show the weakness of the strong, is also to be found in the Anonymus Iamblichi (89.6 D.-K. = 40.6 L.-M.).

Callicles, when pressed by Socrates, will soon relinquish strength as the distinctive criterion for the good and the just (489c). But, in doing so, he strips his theses of their 'realistic' foundation, showing them for what they are: a brilliant yet fruitless rhetorical exercise.[30] Rather, as we shall see in the next chapter, it is in relation to the individual (that is, to moral rather than political problems) that Callicles' ideas prove more compelling: his arguments represent more of 'a life choice, a nostalgia for Homeric times, a hope to free oneself from the bonds of egalitarian morality and law, than a genuine theoretical argument'.[31]

Thrasymachus and political realism

Even though they bear witness to an increasing discontent with democracy (something also attested by many other writings from the same period),[32] Callicles' statements do not pose any real obstacle to the theses in favour of *nomos*, which find their most prominent spokesman in Protagoras. More insidious opponents are to be found in the persons of Thrasymachus and Antiphon, two leading exponents – along with the historian Thucydides – of what in modern terms we might describe as 'political realism'.

Just as for Callicles, Plato's testimony proves both crucial and problematic for Thrasymachus. Although (unlike in Callicles' case) many other sources talk about Thrasymachus, our only source for his political thought is the first book of the *Republic*. Here the sophist is credited with different theses on justice that are difficult to reconcile: first, justice is defined as the advantage of the stronger, 'what is advantageous for the person who is stronger' (*Republic*, 338c = 85B6a D.-K. = 35D21a L.-M.; the thesis is later rephrased as respect for the laws, 340a–b), and then as 'what is good for someone else' (343c = 35D21a L.-M.). Modern scholars have poured out rivers of ink in the attempt to reconcile these theses, without ever reaching a shared solution. Without delving into this complex debate,[33] it may be noted that the ambiguities are

[30] Fussi 2006: 203–20.

[31] Vegetti 2018: 198.

[32] The most significant text, not least because of the numerous affinities it has with the sophists, is the anonymous *Constitution of the Athenians*, with regard to which I will refer to Lapini 1997 and Gray 2007; also very interesting is Xenophon, *Memorabilia*, 1.2.40–6.

[33] For a reconstruction of the different hypotheses that have been put forward (to show either the coherence or the incoherence between the two theses, and to favour one or the other), see

at least partly resolved if we consider the fact that the first thesis refers to more specifically political issues, while the second one concerns individual choices and hence 'ethical' problems (although we should not forget that, prior to Aristotle, the distinction between ethics and politics was not explicitly theorized). Consequently, it is worth focusing here on the first thesis, while the importance of the second thesis – namely, what its polemical target is – will become clear in the next chapter, where we will be discussing happiness.

In arguing with Socrates, or rather in countering his defence of justice, Thrasymachus claims of justice that it is 'what is advantageous for the person who is stronger' (*Republic*, 338c = 85B6a D.-K. = 35D21 L.-M.), noting immediately afterwards that the stronger is to be understood in the sense of 'the established rule' (*arche*): hence, justice 'is the advantage of the stronger', that is of the established rule (*Republic*, 338d–e). This thesis has often been compared to Callicles', but this is a misleading comparison: while it is true that both of them pay much attention to strength, Thrasymachus clearly understands strength in the sense of power, and his emphasis on the theme of power allows him to avoid the conflation between the descriptive and prescriptive aspects that had proven so fatal to Callicles. Thrasymachus' thesis is merely descriptive, insofar as it does not pass any judgement but only records a fact: namely that strength and power constitute a fundamental aspect of human relations. Power is where the strength lies, and both justice and law are subordinate to it: those who are in a position of strength – that is, those who wield power – establish rules and laws, the only purpose of which is to ensure that those in a position of strength preserve their power and hence pursue their own advantage.[34]

Despite the apparent similarities, the theses of Callicles and Thrasymachus differ in some crucial respects. First of all, Thrasymachus' thesis acquires a universal value that Callicles' lacks: it can be used to describe all the political relations that govern human lives, without the need to draw any arbitrary distinctions between good and bad governments. Furthermore – and this is the most significant divergence – Thrasymachus and Callicles have two different conceptions of justice. For Callicles, justice is something real, something that objectively exists and is embedded within reality (*physis*): its

Macé 2009: 159–62 and, most recently, with further bibliography, Barney 2017, Wedgwood 2017, and El Murr 2019.

[34] Vegetti 1998: 240–7.

purpose (a rather confused one, as we have seen) is to bring human *nomos* in line with this natural justice. For Thrasymachus, in contrast, it makes no sense to speak of natural justice: that is, to speak of justice as though it is something that exists independently of human beings. Justice is a purely human concept, which is not rooted in *physis* at all; it is a convention that regulates human relations (and does so according to power relations).

These clarifications help us to better understand the relation between Thrasymachus and Protagoras, who probably represents the polemical target of the former's thesis: Thrasymachus' realism is developed within the same framework as Protagoras' conventionalism, so much so that one could argue that the affinities between the two are greater than those between Thrasymachus and Callicles. However, the conclusions reached by Thrasymachus overturn the meaning of Protagoras' thesis, highlighting its limits and the problems that it poses. What the two sophists have in common is their starting point, positivism – a rather widespread idea in the Greek world.[35] According to this assumption, there is no justice outside law: only what the laws decree to be just is just. Yet the identification of law with justice does not guarantee the correctness of Protagoras' reasoning, since alongside law and justice, or rather behind them, there lies power; and the acknowledgement of the priority of power leads to opposite conclusions from those of Protagoras. According to the latter, as we have seen, it is the community as a whole that establishes the rules, laws, and values that promote peaceful coexistence and the pursuit of everyone's interests. According to Thrasymachus, by contrast, the idea of a harmonious and close-knit community is an illusion, since all human communities are created on the basis of power relations that govern them: society is nothing but different parts jostling for power. This entails a different evaluation of *nomos*, justice, and interests. Laws are not the result of a collective action: more crudely, they depend on the choices and interests of the group that finds itself in a dominant position. Therefore, to the extent that law is identified with the laws, it is a product of force; it represents not a shared value capable of neutralizing potential conflicts in the community, but a partisan means to legitimize a given balance of power between the members of the community. In modern terms, to

[35] Vegetti 1998: 240–2.

borrow Marxist terminology, we might speak of justice as an ideology which offers a false view of reality, so as to justify the partisan reality of power through the screen of a universal principle.

The same considerations also apply to what is useful. For Protagoras as much as Thrasymachus, advantageousness is the motive behind all political decisions. However, given that the decisions are always made by a part of society rather than the whole, it follows that advantageousness does not concern the community as a whole, but only those who find themselves in a stronger position, and who endorse as what is just their own private interests, which is to say what is advantageous for the preservation of their own power (hence, in 343c, Thrasymachus will argue that justice is 'what is good for someone else': the good of the one who is in power, not of the one who is ruled).

On a more concretely political level, it may be noted that Thrasymachus distances himself from democracy, yet in a different way from Callicles' frontal attack. One consequence of Thrasymachus' realist, objective, and detached attitude is that it would make no sense to draw a distinction between good and bad regimes, because every form of government is simply the implementation of a power relation, which it would be pointless to criticize: democracy is no less legitimate than aristocracy or monarchy (*Republic*, 338e–339a). Upon closer inspection, however, it is easy to see that this apparent legitimation of the democratic regime actually conflicts with the assumptions of the champions of democracy. The main postulate behind the democratic theory – as may be inferred from Protagoras or Pericles – is the belief that democracy is the government of everyone, and not just of a part; and it is precisely in this universal character of democracy that its specificity and superiority lie: as the government of everyone, democracy is the only regime which can ensure everyone's good and advantage. Thrasymachus' analyses disprove these ideas: insofar as democracy is the government of a part of society, albeit the majority, it follows that it only safeguards the interests of that part and not of everyone. When Thrasymachus associates the democratic regime with the more traditional ones of aristocracy and monarchy, all he is doing is once again proving the centrality of power in human relations (since every form of government expresses a power relation), without making any concessions to the alleged merits or specificity of democratic government.

Antiphon and the logic of the individual

While Thrasymachus brought to light the inconsistencies of positivism, even more scathing observations were put forward by Antiphon, who opposed the logic of the individual to the Protagorean logic of the community. The juxtaposition between Thrasymachus and Antiphon might seem surprising, as Antiphon is usually reckoned among the champions of *physis* – unlike Thrasymachus, whose analysis is entirely developed within a positivist and conventionalist context, which entails no reference to objective or natural values.[36] However, as we have seen in Chapter 2, this alleged opposition is actually a fallacious one: according to Antiphon, nature is neutral and does not provide any normative values. This is the truth of his work *On Truth*. The same considerations also apply to fragment 44, again from *On Truth*, which more specifically concerns human *physis*.[37] In an apparently trivial way, but actually drawing upon the anatomical research of physicians and other scientists, Antiphon sets out to systematically classify the various limbs and organs of human bodies, along with the functions associated with them (87B44A, 2.15–3.12 D.-K. = 37D38b L.-M.). The outcome is an acknowledgement of the biological equality of human beings. Yet, contrary to what one might assume, this biological equality does not have any humanitarian consequences: it is not the source of any rights, nor does it lay the foundations for political equality, against the conventions that divide people (such as the distinction between free men and slaves, or nobles and non-nobles). On the contrary, the consequences drawn from this acknowledgement entail serious problems: equality means that humans have the same needs, and this gives rise to a potentially conflictual situation, whereby all people desire the same things and each person pursues his or her own interests against those of others.

This analysis of human *physis* goes hand in hand with – and sets the ground for – that of *nomos*: the lengthy papyrus fragment that makes up

[36] This juxtaposition might seem even more surprising if we consider the fact that most scholars tend to interpret Antiphon not just as a champion of *physis* but as the first spokesman for natural justice. However, this reading is based on an erroneous reconstruction of the papyrus transmitting 87B44 D.-K. (=37D38b L.-M.), as may be inferred from the recent discovery of another part of the same papyrus: see the edition of Bastianini and Caizzi 1989 (which I follow for the column order) and the point made by Narcy 1996.

[37] In my analysis of this fragment, I am partly drawing upon Bonazzi 2020, which I refer to for further bibliographical references. Ostwald 1990 remains the most useful introduction.

fragment 44 preserves the most in-depth analysis of the problematic relations between these two concepts. For Antiphon, *nomos*, in all of its meanings (as law, tradition, and custom), is something negative: a 'bond' that seeks to regulate what nature has left unregulated, thereby preventing individuals from fulfilling their needs or desires (87B44B, 1.22–4.8 D.-K. = 37D38a, 1.22–4.8 L.-M.). This attempt to control *physis* inevitably proves unfavourable, since it prevents us from pursuing our own advantage, which always depends on our nature, on our constitution:

> If one reasons correctly, what causes pain does not help nature more than what causes pleasures; and so what causes pain would not be more beneficial either than what pleases. For what is truly beneficial must not be harmful but helpful.
>
> (87B44B, 4.9–22 D.-K. = 37D38a, 4.9–22 L.-M.)

With Antiphon, the opposition between *physis* and *nomos* becomes explicit and clear-cut.

At this stage, however, one could raise the following objection: given the neutral character of *physis* and the potential for conflict among humans, *nomos* might be seen to have a positive value insofar as it is capable of preventing the war of all against all. A solution of this kind is implicit in the aforementioned thesis put forward by Lycophron (83.3 D.-K. = 38D3 L.-M.) and finds an eloquent formulation in the long speech that Plato puts in his brother Glaucon's mouth in the second book of the *Republic* (358e–359c). By nature, humans tend to commit acts of injustice towards one another; but, realizing that in this situation the advantages are fewer than the disadvantages, they established a corpus of laws to regulate their actions, depriving them of certain possibilities, yet ensuring security. In other words, the bonds to which we are subjected also restrain brutes and predators far worse than us.

The following section of the Antiphon passage precisely addresses objections of this sort: a careful analysis of social dynamics shows that *nomos* is often incapable of ensuring this security. Despite its coercive power, *nomos* is incapable of preventing its own violation: for example, it decrees that stealing is forbidden, but does not actually prevent everyone from stealing. This leads to a paradoxical situation, insofar as *nomos* proves doubly disadvantageous precisely for those who respect it:

> If the laws provided some help for those who submit to such situations, and loss for those who do not submit to them but who oppose them, [col. 6] it would not be useless

to obey the laws. But as it is, it is evident that, for those who submit to such situations, a just outcome deriving from a law is not enough to provide them help. First, it permits the sufferer to suffer and the doer to do. And just as, at that time [i.e. before the crime] it did not prevent either the sufferer from suffering or the doer from doing, so too when reference is made to it for the purpose of punishment, it is not more on the side of the one who has suffered than on that of the one who has done. For it is necessary that he persuade those people who will exact punishment that he has suffered, or that he be capable of obtaining justice by deceit. But the doer too is permitted to deny the same things [col. 7]...exactly as much of a defence is available to the defendant, as the accusation that is available to the accuser, and persuasiveness is balanced for the one who has suffered and for the one who has done.

(87B44B, 5.25–7.14 D.-K. = 37D38a, 5.25–7.14 L.-M.)

Let us keep to the example of stealing. Those who accept the injunction not to steal will not steal, even in a situation in which stealing might fulfil a need (as in the case of those who are hungry and steal food). This is one disadvantage; but, what is more, respecting the law does not protect one from the possibility of being in turn robbed by those who do not respect this law. Consequently, one risks suffering an additional drawback, which adds insult to injury, considering that the law courts assign equal rights to the victim and to the guilty party, and that the outcome of a trial depends more on the capacity to persuade than on the ascertainment of the truth.

No less interesting are the analyses devoted to the practice of bearing witness in relation to the problem of justice (87B44C D.-K. = 37D38c L.-M.).[38] People usually believe that it is unjust to commit injustices against those who have not committed any injustice; and that it is just to testify to the truth in a court case. But, according to Antiphon, these two beliefs are mutually incompatible when a truthful witness leads to the sentencing of a criminal who had not done that witness any wrong. Moreover, Antiphon observes, in doing so the witness puts themself at risk, since he antagonizes someone – the criminal – who will sooner or later seek revenge. All this brings out the limits of *nomos*, which not only prevents people from fulfilling their primary needs, but is even incapable of protecting those who yield to its rule. It is as though *physis* and *nomos* are applied at two parallel levels: the level of truth and that of opinion, the level of concreteness and that of abstraction, without these levels ever really meeting. While through his or her action the witness has upheld the *nomos* of an abstract

[38] See Furley 1981.

community, he or she has caused, and has incurred, concrete and personal damages.

Antiphon's analyses are important in several respects. First of all, it is worth noting that they constitute an eloquent example of the sophists' wide range of interests. It is generally assumed that the sophists had no interest whatsoever in the research conducted by natural philosophers and scientists, and that they only dealt with politics. Antiphon's case instead presents us with a more nuanced situation: the originality and importance of the sophists rather lies in their ability to bring together the two spheres, and to put scientific research to the service of political aims. This is a matter of method as well as content: the adoption of a detached and scientific, descriptive and non-judgemental attitude is what lends shape to the 'realistic' approach, which constitutes one of the most significant contributions offered by the sophists' political reflection.

It is crucial to take account of this 'realistic' and detached attitude if we are to fully understand Antiphon's position: the text clearly suggests that Antiphon did not wish to present his own conception of justice in opposition to conventional ones, as Callicles does in the *Gorgias*. Rather, his primary aim is to closely engage with the theories of justice that were then circulating in Athens and in the Greek world more widely. In particular, the opening lines of the fragment show that the sophist was particularly interested in addressing the positivist thesis, which had been developed in particularly compelling terms by Protagoras: the definition of justice as obedience to the laws of the community of which one is a citizen (87B44B, 1.6–11 D.-K. = 37D38a, 1.6–11 L.-M.) clearly captures the cornerstone of this thesis, namely the identification of law with justice (what is just is what the laws decree).

As we have just seen, the critique of positivism is common to many sophists. However, Antiphon is the one who best grasps the underlying crux of the matter by raising the vital question of the foundation of the law (and hence of justice): if justice is a human convention, meaning that it simply consists of the laws established by people, what authoritativeness or foundation can it have? Protagoras' answer, as we have seen, is the idea of what is useful. The authority and legitimacy of *nomos* depend on its capacity to ensure everyone's interests: this is the reason why *nomos* must be respected. Nevertheless, a concrete analysis of how society works shows the flimsiness of Protagoras' answer, which is an abstract one, insofar as he refers to a (ideal) community of citizens rather than to the concrete needs and interests of individuals. Often (2.26–7) the law entails coercion without offering any advantages or security. What are we to do in these cases? Antiphon pushes the positivist thesis towards a paradoxical conclusion: if the legitimacy of *nomos* depends on the advantages it provides, if the foundation of justice is its usefulness, and if in certain cases it is more useful to violate justice than it is to respect it, it follows that injustice is just – or at any rate, and more pragmatically, that one should publicly abide by the law but secretly follow nature. Antiphon's reasoning should not be interpreted as a call to go against the law; rather, it is a provocation that pushes to its extreme (and unexpected) consequences a widespread idea of justice, which had been strongly championed by Protagoras:

> Therefore justice is not to transgress against the legal institutions of whatever city one happens to be a citizen of. So a man would make use of justice in the way that would be most advantageous for himself if, in the presence of witnesses, he considered that it is the laws that are great, but, alone and without witnesses, that it is what belong to nature. For what belongs to the laws is adventitious, but what belongs to nature is necessary. And what belongs to the laws is the product of an agreement, but what belongs to nature is the product of nature, not of an agreement. [col. 2] So if someone transgresses against legal institutions without being noticed by those who agreed upon them, he escapes shame and punishment; but if they notice, he does not. But if, contravening what is possible, he does violence to anything produced by nature, the harm is no less if no man notices him, and it is not greater if all men see him. For it is not because of opinion that he is harmed, but because of the truth.
>
> (87B44B, 1.5–2.23 D.-K. = 37D38a, 1.5–2.23 L.-M.)

Certainly, Antiphon's analyses present many similarities to Thrasymachus' thesis, which they usefully integrate: while the latter had criticized the legitimacy of positivism starting from the problem of power, Antiphon reaches similar conclusions by setting out from the problem of usefulness. If anything, Antiphon's analysis is even more radical: Thrasymachus was operating on a distinctly political level, by considering the division of the city into social strata (the people vs nobles for instance). Antiphon instead appears to be interested in a more 'philosophical' analysis, which he extends down to the ultimate constituent of the city, individuals. It is here that the choice of Protagoras as a polemical target becomes clear. Whereas in his myth Protagoras had described human beings as 'not yet social' to show that his interests are eminently social (the human being is a political animal: there is no human who is not a citizen, a member of a group), Antiphon analyses the life of humans in society to show that his interests are individual and hence anti-social – in other words, they concern the human as an individual and not as a citizen. This explains the limits of Protagoras' defence of *nomos*: the only reality is each individual,[39] whereas the laws of the *polis*, directed as they are at an abstract citizen community, at most express an external and artificial consensus, incapable of safeguarding the natural and hence real interests of individuals.[40]

Such is the 'truth' that Antiphon reaches through an impartial analysis of reality, and it is a truth that affords few illusions as to the possibility of building a just and close-knit society. The dominant tone of his analysis suggests an acknowledgement of the difficult condition of humanity, caught between natural needs and social constrictions.[41] However, this is not to say that it is impossible to live in a satisfying way. After all, the human being has a most valuable means to make up for the limits of politics and *nomos*, a means which unfortunately he or she rarely resorts to: intelligence. As we shall see in the next chapter, it is by using one's intelligence that it is possible to find a balance both within oneself and with others.

Other enemies of *nomos*

Before wrapping up this long discussion, brief mention must be made of other testimonies which can be traced back to the sophists' debates and which record positions akin to those of Thrasymachus and Antiphon. One interesting parallel is to be found in a tragedy by Critias, the *Pirithous*:

[39] Hourcade 2001: 115.

[40] Farrar 1988: 115–18. In passing, it goes without saying that these conclusions have anti-democratic implications. Naturally, by this I do not mean to say that it is possible to infer from the surviving fragments of Antiphon's *On Truth* that he openly sided against democracy: on the contrary, what makes Antiphon's analyses so intriguing is his claim that he is not taking any stand himself, but wishes the dynamics of natural and social reality to emerge on their own. Still, it must be noted that his analyses of humans and society, his systematic emphasis on the essentially anti-social character of human beings, and hence his privileging of the needs of the individual over the collective rights of citizens constitute one of the most dangerous attacks on Athenian democracy, which was founded on the identification of the common good with the interests of individuals. The 'atomization' of common interest into many private and mutually conflicting interests amounts to the de facto impossibility of finding the kind of common good which, in the eyes of Protagoras and Pericles, was the distinguishing trait of democracy.

[41] Decleva Caizzi 1999: 327.

An honest character is surer than the law:
For the former, no orator could ever pervert it;
While the latter, he often ruins it
By agitating it up and down with his speeches.
(88B22 D.-K. = Dram. T67 L.-M.)

Undoubtedly, this combined criticism of the law and rhetoric, which is typical of Athenian assemblies, offers additional proof of the growing dissatisfaction that, in the second half of the fifth century, many intellectuals displayed towards *nomos*, which was increasingly identified with democratic *nomos*. But it should also be noted that, in these verses, the criticism of rhetoric amounts to an attempt to distance oneself from sophistry: again, Critias emerges not so much as a sophist as a writer capable of exploiting some sophistic themes for his polemical purposes.[42]

Even more interesting is another testimony from *Sisyphus*, a satyr-play previously attributed to Critias but more likely to be the work of Euripides.[43] Some significant analogies with Antiphon may be found: *nomos* is assigned an instrumental value, as a means to safeguard communities. Yet this value is denied at the very moment in which it is posited: laws were introduced to bring an end to the bestial violence that originally marked human life; however, these laws only partially met their aim, because people continued to secretly commit injustices, thereby undermining society. Only the invention of the gods as omniscient and omnipotent controllers laid the foundations for a more stable society. Leaving aside the issue of the invention of the gods, on which we will focus in Chapter 6, the similarities with Antiphon's idea of the conventional character of *nomos* and its weakness are undoubtedly significant.[44]

What is more difficult to assess is Hippias' position, as it emerges from two testimonies from Plato's *Protagoras* (337c–e = 86C1 D.-K. = 36D17 L.-M.) and Xenophon's *Memorabilia* (4.4.5–25, only partly included by Diels among the testimonies on Hippias as 86A14 D.-K.; =36D11 L.-M.). In both passages Hippias emerges as a staunch critic of *nomos*, which is accused of imposing arbitrary distinctions

[42] See H. Patzer 1974. Critias' aims are quite clear: an unrelenting struggle against democracy, in an attempt to import into Athens the values of the oligarchic ideology of Sparta. On this, see Bultrighini 1999 and Iannucci 2002.

[43] See Chapter 6, p. 119.

[44] Ostwald 1986: 282.

against nature (86C1 D.-K. = 36D17 L.-M.: *nomos* 'which is a tyrant over men, commits violence upon many things against nature') and of having an unstable character (*Mem.* 4.4.14: 'Laws can hardly be thought of much account, or observance of them, seeing that the very men who passed them often reject and amend them'). These are essentially similar objections to those raised by Antiphon and *Sisyphus*. According to some scholars, moreover, both Xenophon and Plato present Hippias as a resolute champion of *physis*, or even as the theorizer of the existence of a divine and/or natural justice.[45] However, it is more prudent to suspend judgement on this interpretation: with regard to Xenophon's *Memorabilia*, because the idea of a divine justice is something that is rather upheld by Socrates;[46] and with regard to Plato, because the reference to *physis* is probably to be understood in a more restricted sense, as we shall see in the next section. The testimonies we have, then, allows us to identify Hippias too as a critic of *nomos*, even though it is impossible to clearly determine what his overall stance was on the thorny problem of justice (assuming that he indeed took a stance on the matter).

The problem of equality

Another strongly debated topic was equality. Once again, the political context – the ups and downs of Athenian democracy – helps us to understand the interest in this issue: two of the catchwords of the democratic regime, those which best represented this form of government, were *isegoria* and *isonomia*, which is to say everyone's right to express themselves and everyone's equality before the law (notwithstanding the fact that 'everyone' excluded a considerable section of society[47]). Moreover, the importance of the topic is confirmed by the fact that discussions about equality extended to broader fields, touching upon social, racial, and economic questions.[48] Naturally, as in the case of justice, the topic was addressed by many different authors, and not just sophists, but the latter's contribution was often highly original

[45] Untersteiner 1954: 278–83.
[46] Decleva Caizzi 1985: 203–8, has hypothesized that Socrates' thesis specifically has Antiphon as its polemical target.
[47] See p. 73, n. 19.
[48] Guthrie 1971: 148–63.

and raised some crucial questions. Usually, the sophists' position on this issue has been invoked in support of an 'Enlightenment' interpretation of their thought, presenting them as the first thinkers to ever emphasize the need to truly free oneself from the prejudices oppressing people's lives. The surviving testimonies, however, suggest a more restrained evaluation: certainly, many sophists must be credited with having brought some real problems up for discussion. Yet here too many of them would appear to have been driven not so much by the need to 'rouse men from dogmatic slumber', as by a desire to investigate certain problems and topics – and perhaps too by a wish to provoke the public by going against the grain.

One interesting example of the sophists' attitude to these problems is provided by Antiphon, who in *On Truth* states that 'we are all fitted similarly by nature in all regards to be both barbarians and Greeks' (87B44A, 2.10–15 D.-K. = 37D38b, 2.10–15 L.-M.). Many have been inspired by this statement to attribute egalitarian or democratic ideas to Antiphon. But the passage is open to other readings as well. The reference to barbarians is actually used to deliver a subtle polemical attack on the inconsistencies of the Greeks, who, while respecting their gods and laws, display the same prejudices of which they accuse barbarians: in doing so, Antiphon notes, 'we have become barbarians toward each other' (87B44A, 2.7–10 D.-K. = 37D38b, 2.7–10 L.-M.). Apparently, this claim does not put forward any positive view of barbarians; rather, in order to achieve the desired effect, it must imply a negative evaluation: to criticize his interlocutors' behaviour, Antiphon adopts their perspective and shows that they (be they Greeks or Athenians) behave exactly like the people they claim to despise. The reference to barbarians serves an instrumental and polemical purpose: it is used to stigmatize the incoherent conduct of the people with whom Antiphon is polemically engaging. But this polemic can hardly be taken as evidence of his role as a champion of the equality between barbarians and Greeks.[49]

A no less delicate matter is the evaluation of another two testimonies, concerning Hippias and Lycophron. In the aforementioned passage of

[49] Decleva Caizzi 1986b. Antiphon's polemic becomes even more significant if, as seems likely, the sophist and the oligarchical rhetor were one and the same person: in this case, Antiphon would have criticized slavery not on humanitarian grounds, but in order to once again highlight the limits 'of the lame egalitarianism of the democratic *polis*' (Canfora 2001: 215).

the *Protagoras*, Hippias addresses the following words to the other characters of the dialogue:

I consider that you all belong to the same family, household, and city – by nature (*physis*), not by law (or convention, *nomos*): for what is similar belongs by nature to the same family as what is similar, whereas law (or convention, *nomos*), which is tyrant over men, commits violence upon many things against nature.

(86C1 D.-K. = 36D17 L.-M.)

Aristotle informs us that Lycophron criticized the nobility, arguing that 'the beauty of nobility is invisible, dignity exists in speech' (83.4 D.-K. = 38D4 L.-M.). As in Hippias' case, this polemic against nobility, which is depreciated as a mere name with no basis in reality, finds its starting point in the opposition between *nomos* and *physis* (of which the opposition between reality and words is a variant). Certainly, upon a first reading one gets a strong impression that both authors are defending the cause of the natural equality of human beings; moreover, this is what many authoritative scholars have argued. But perhaps it should not be ruled out that this 'bold outlook on the old principles of the "noble stock"' is aimed not at a democratic defence of the rights of all people but rather at 'replacing one kind of inequality with an inequality of an even more radical kind: what we have is the praise of the new superiority, and supremacy, of intelligence'.[50]

Gorgias and Thrasymachus are credited instead with two stances in favour of the equality of the Greeks against the barbarians: 'trophies won from the barbarians demand hymns, those from the Greeks dirges' (Gorgias in the *Funeral Oration*, 82B5b D.-K. = 32D29 L.-M.); 'Shall we, who are Greeks, be slaves to Archelaus, who is a barbarian?' (Thrasymachus in the oration *For the Larissians*, 85B2 D.-K. = 35D18 L.-M.). Yet it is almost certain that these are extemporary claims, instrumental to the political speeches of which they are part:

The *Funeral Oration*, which he [*sc.* Gorgias] pronounced in Athens, was delivered on those men who had fallen in the wars, whom the Athenian buried at public expenses with eulogies; it is composed with extraordinary skill. For given that he wanted to rouse the Athenians against the Medes and the Persians and was arguing with the same intention as in his *Olympic Oration*, he said nothing at all about concord among the Greeks, since he was speaking to Athenians (who desired supremacy, which could only achieved by choosing a very energetic policy), but instead he praised

[50] Isnardi Parente 1977: 32–3.

at length the trophies won from the Medes, telling them that 'trophies won from the barbarians demand hymns, those from the Greeks dirges'.

(82A1 D.-K. = 32D27 and R19 L.-M.)

As far as Thrasymachus is concerned, his pan-Hellenic plea was directed against the expansionist aims of Archelaus, a Macedonian whom it would have been an exaggeration to regard as a barbarian.[51] Finally, Alcidamas is credited with a resolute stance against slavery: 'god has set all men free; nature has made no man slave' (fr. 19). But in this case, too, we are dealing with a sentence taken from an oration (to be more precise, a school exercise): it is likely to be a catchy line, designed more to capture the public's attention than to defend the abolitionist cause.

In other words, an adequate contextualization of existing testimonies often suggests that it would be unwarranted to consider the sophists champions of human rights, by attributing to them a kind of awareness that would only be fully developed over the course of the centuries. At the same time, however, we should not go from one extreme to the other, by concluding that their reflections have no value whatsoever. Ultimately, driven by their eagerness to critically examine prejudices and commonplaces, the sophists established themselves as the first thinkers to expound theses of universal value, destined to have untold consequences: 'the struggle was destined to be long, but it had begun'.[52] And this is no small feat.

The enduring relevance of the sophists

The sophists' discussions of the controversial phenomenon of justice constitute a striking refutation of the interpretations of those scholars who were only willing to acknowledge their importance in the field of rhetoric. On the contrary, the significance of the problem of *logos* can only be fully appreciated by framing it within a practical and political context. Only at this stage can we grasp the sophistic movement in all of its complexity. Moreover, only at this stage can we measure its relevance with respect to our own world and interests. The contemporary age is marked by a loss of foundations (or, rather, by the awareness

[51] Bonazzi 2008: 66–8.
[52] Guthrie 1971: 160.

that there are no foundations); and this problem requires a practical as well as a theoretical response. If this is the case, we are bound to acknowledge the profoundness of the sophists, who were the first to investigate such problems.

Even more relevant is the way in which the sophists tackled them: whatever the thesis upheld, or the sophist involved, what distinguishes their approach is their underlying realism – the disenchanted gaze of someone who is not searching for easy justifications. Truly, it is difficult not to agree with Nietzsche's criticism of George Grote, who defended the sophists by portraying them as perfect Victorian gentlemen. The sophists' chief merit – or limit, depending on one's point of view – is their realism:

> The sophists are no more than realists...Grote's tactics in defence of the Sophists are false: he wants to raise them to the rank of men of honor and ensigns of morality – but it was their honor not to indulge in any swindle with big words and virtues.[53]

Similar considerations, as we shall see, apply to another two topics that are still constantly debated: happiness and the gods, or religion.

[53] Nietzsche 1964: 249.

V TEACHING VIRTUE: THE SOPHISTS ON HAPPINESS AND SUCCESS

One frequently overlooked aspect of the sophists' reflection concerns the kind of problems that today might be included in an ethical treatise, such as happiness and pleasure. Usually it is claimed that the sophists shifted the focus of enquiry from nature to the human world, but then the emphasis is almost exclusively placed on the political side of these investigations (which is no doubt significant, as we have seen in the previous chapter). This is a misleading perspective, which applies modern conceptual schemes to the ancient world, creating distortions and misunderstandings. Before Aristotle, there is no point in distinguishing between the ethical and the political spheres, since ethics and politics ultimately constitute two aspects of the same problem: how to reach fulfilment and thus lead a happy life. Certainly, in order to answer this question it is necessary to embark on an analysis of political problems, such as justice or the best form of government: the fact that human beings live together is something that must be taken into account. But the ultimate goal is self-realization. This is the end towards which everyone tends.

In the fifth-century debate, the issue at stake was that of *arete*, a term which is usually translated as 'virtue': how can one become virtuous? In our day, given our idea of virtue, a question of this sort may not seem very pertinent, and one might object that virtue is rather an obstacle to self-realization. For the Greeks, however, *arete* primarily indicates a capacity to perform, which enables individuals to exercise their function or task in the best possible way: it is the quality (or range of qualities) that helps one to stand out from one's group and to fully realize one's potential, justifying one's superiority over all others and earning the individual admiration, along with material goods. An alternative translation of *arete*, which better conveys this underlying meaning, is 'excellence'. At the risk of oversimplifying things, the problem might be then redefined in terms of success: how can one obtain success, so as to lead a gratifying and happy life? This is an ever-relevant question, which the Greeks never ceased to address.

In Greece, moreover, the debate on this issue was made even more heated by the new social and cultural conditions which had emerged in the fifth century. Whereas in the previous ages, dominated by the aristocratic outlook, the prevalent thesis had been that a person's 'value' derives from their natural endowments, which they need to cultivate by following their ancestors' example,[1] in the fifth century, with the rise of democracy, the belief took root that anyone could attain virtue. This made the problem of education and teaching an even more pressing one. Everyone could become 'virtuous', which is to say develop qualities that would propel them to the summit of the community; the problem, then, was to learn how to attain virtue. And this is precisely what the sophists promised to teach, starting from Protagoras, who claimed that what people could learn from him was 'good deliberation about household matters, to know how to manage one's own household in the best way possible, and about those of the city, so as to be most capable of acting and speaking in the city's interests' (*Protagoras*, 318b = 80A5 D.-K. = 31D37 L.-M.). In other words, Protagoras promised to teach people virtue (*Protagoras*, 319b; see also 349a and *Meno*, 91a). Plato reports that Gorgias instead mocked those who promised to teach others virtue (*Meno*, 95b = 82A21 D.-K. = 32D47 L.-M., quoted above, p. 75). Yet the purpose of his teaching was much the same (see e.g. Plato, *Gorgias*, 452d–e).[2] No less significantly, even one of the *Dissoi logoi*, the sixth, is entirely devoted to refuting the thesis that 'wisdom and virtue can neither be taught nor learned' (90.6.1 D.-K. = 40.6.1 L.-M.). Once again, then, the sophists prove capable of grasping and addressing the most important problems of the life of the city, eliciting opposite reactions – enthusiasm or aversion – through their bold claims.

Generally speaking, a defining feature of the sophists' reflection is the affirmation of the priority of the individual over the community. The sources we have all appear to go in this direction, with one significant exception: Protagoras. Unlike the other sophists, Protagoras seems to be striving to reconcile the interests of the individual with those of the public sphere, by emphasizing the eminently political dimension of human nature. In this he once again shows significant affinities with the democratic ideology of Pericles, and I will therefore refer back to the previous chapter for a more detailed exposition of his ideas. In all other cases, what makes the sophists' analyses interesting

[1] See, for example, Theognis, lines 27 ff.; Pindar, *Olympian Odes*, 2.86, 9.100, 10.20.

[2] Also revealing, in this respect, is an epigram from Olympia that was written in his honour: 'No mortal ever invented a finer art than Gorgias / To exercise the soul in competition of excellence. / And it is of him that, in Apollo's hollows, the statue is dedicated, / A paradigm not of wealth, but of the piety of his character' (82A8 D.-K. = 32P34b L.-M.).

is their awareness of the problematic bond between each individual and his or her community. Usually this leads to the (predictable) charge that the sophists promote social egoism: their criticism that justice and the law only possess conventional value, the doubts they repeatedly raise concerning the existence of the gods – who were traditionally regarded as the bastions of order and goodness – and their constant references to personal interest may well be seen to expose them to the charge of immoralism. No doubt, the sophists tackled some thorny social questions, adopting an ambiguous stance vis-à-vis traditional values, in a subtle play of rejection and adoption. But, while the destructive aspect of their reflections is what most captures our attention, we should not overlook the many sources that inform us of how they also put forward some positive suggestions. The picture of the sophists as 'immoralists' is probably a misrepresentation of their positions, the outcome of a superficial application of certain theses that have not been adequately understood, and which must be taken into account without making them the one and only object of the sophists' reflection.[3]

The immoralists

The idea that the sophists' teaching amounted to a sort of immoralism which justified any action whatsoever was a common one in fifth- and fourth-century Athens, and finds authoritative confirmation in Aristophanes and Plato.[4] Arguably the most eloquent testimony is provided by the *Clouds*, in which Aristophanes unleashes his comic fury on all the representatives of the new culture – not just the sophists, but also natural philosophers and even Socrates, who constitutes the real polemical target of the comedy. The central point made by the *Clouds* is that the responsibility for the ruin of Athens ultimately falls on the new 'doctrines' promoted by these self-styled masters, doctrines which lead to (and justify) the most subversive act of all for the order of the city: a son beating his father. From a social point of view, this is also a generational clash, which takes the form of a rejection on the part of the new generations of those principles that had made the city of Athens great.[5]

[3] See Bett 2002.

[4] A detailed overview of these testimonies may be found in De Romilly 1988: 194–231; see also Chapter 1, pp. 8–9.

[5] Ostwald 1986: 229–50.

Compared to Aristophanes, Plato adopts a more nuanced and hence more interesting position. First of all, it is worth noting that his polemic seems to be more restricted: while, generally speaking, his dialogues deliver an all-round attack against the sophists, when it comes to ethical questions it is almost invariably Gorgias who is made the central target. This is rather perplexing, considering that Gorgias even denied that he dealt with virtue and claimed to confine his teaching to the art of speech (consider the aforementioned testimony 82A21 D.-K. = 32D47 L.-M.). Plato, however, may have been right in a sense: for it is precisely on account of his alleged 'neutrality' that Gorgias might be accused of being a bad teacher.[6] Indeed, according to Plato, what makes Gorgias dangerous as a teacher is the fact that, on the one hand, he refuses to address moral issues but, on the other, promises to teach how to achieve success: the combination of these two elements may be exploited as a means to justify egoism, whereby the only thing that matters is the pursuit of one's goals, regardless of other people's point of view, needs, and rights. This is precisely the criticism formulated by Plato, who accused Gorgias not of any moral shortcomings (besides, the sources portray Gorgias as a sober and moderate man), but on account of the noxious consequences of his teaching.

Particularly revealing, in this respect, is the presentation of two pupils of Gorgias – Meno in the dialogue of the same name, and Callicles in the *Gorgias* – offering two different versions of the same problem: a subdued version and a radical one. Meno is a fine example of the first type, that of the shy pupil, who is eager to obtain the success that Gorgias has promised him, but who is afraid of taking an open stance against shared values such as justice. This results in a constant oscillation between the egotistic pursuit of what might promote his self-interest and a surface acknowledgement of traditional values. Hence, Meno goes round in circles, without daring to pursue what is implicit in Gorgias' promises (the achievement of success) to its ultimate consequences, yet also without understanding what might make traditional values legitimate.[7]

[6] See also Trabattoni 2000: 19–21.

[7] In the *Gorgias*, a character who is presented in much the same light as Meno is Polus of Acragas, historically another pupil of Gorgias and the author of a treatise on rhetoric. See, for instance, Nails 2002: 252.

Callicles' case is different, since he lacks neither courage nor frankness. He is mostly known for his 'political' theories, which emphasize the rule of force and the superiority of 'the best'.[8] As we have seen, it is easy to show that these are only rhetorical quips, with no coherent content. However, as Nietzsche clearly grasped, the same ideas acquire a very different significance when viewed in relation to the life choices of individuals. Struggling to reach an agreement with Callicles on the issue of who 'the best' might be on the political level, Socrates tries to shift the debate to the individual level: granting for the sake of argument that 'the best' have the right to rule 'the weak', Socrates asks Callicles how 'the best' ought to behave towards themselves, whether they ought to control themselves or not (*Gorgias*, 490e–491e). Callicles initially does not understand Socrates, but then rejects his idea. His reply perfectly illustrates what, according to Plato, was the moral sickness of Athens:

> How could a man prove to be happy if he's enslaved to anyone at all? Rather, this is what's admirable and just by nature – and I'll say it to you now with all frankness – that the man who'll live correctly ought to allow his own appetites to get as large as possible and not restrain them. And when they are as large as possible, he ought to be competent to devote himself to them by virtue of his bravery and intelligence, and to fill them with whatever he may have an appetite for at the time. But this isn't possible for the many, I believe; hence, they become detractors of people like this because of the shame they feel, while they conceal their own impotence. ... The truth of it, Socrates – the thing you claim to pursue – is like this: wantonness, lack of discipline, and freedom, if available in good supply, are excellence and happiness; as for these other things, these fancy phrases, these contracts of men that go against nature, they're worthless nonsense! (Plato, *Gorgias*, 491e–c)

The human being's innermost nature lies in their desiderative component, in the urges and passions that stir within them: it is there, in the capacity to fulfil the needs and desires of one's true self, that the quest for happiness is conducted, against the conventions and limits of traditional morality. While Nietzsche was to appreciate this answer, it was overturned by Plato, who later on in the dialogue redefined it as a defence of radical hedonism and refuted it as such – as a potentially beastly solution and one utterly incapable of explaining what makes a life truly excellent and worth living.

In its radical nature, however, Callicles' challenge raises substantial problems which Plato was well aware of and which he never ceased

[8] See Chapter 4, pp. 77–80.

to investigate.[9] First of all, it must be noted that Callicles is promoting an extreme yet not utterly alien view of traditional morality, which ever since Homer's *Iliad* had rested on the logic of competitiveness and on the friend/enemy dialectic. In particular, it is important to bear in mind that, whether we share Callicles' perspective or not, his challenge may be interpreted as a particularly disturbing confirmation of a problem that always needs to be addressed, that of obligation: why should I limit my legitimate pursuit of happiness out of respect for others?[10]

This is the underlying question which drives the sophists' reflection, as well as that of other Platonic characters, such as the aforementioned Thrasymachus and Glaucon, who newly address the issue in some memorable pages of the *Republic* (Rep. 343a–344a and 358b–361d). If happiness is the ultimate goal of human life, and respect for others is a cause of unhappiness, then how are we to conduct ourselves? Clearly, this is a dangerous question, and the frankness with which the sophists posed it might create the impression that they did so in order to promote theses such as that of Callicles. Yet Callicles' 'immoralist' solution, his invitation to escape 'moral captivity', is only one possible answer. We do not know what solution Gorgias offered: in all likelihood he offered no solution, in the sense that – as we have seen – Gorgias avoided addressing problems of this sort. However, the sources that we have provide information on two other sophists, Antiphon and Prodicus; and they suggest that they were not immoralists, but at most realists and utilitarians.

Antiphon's morality of concord

Not unlike Thrasymachus or Glaucon, Antiphon was well aware of the urgency of the questions just mentioned. As we have seen in Chapter 4, the problem of how to relate to the law and other people was one of the underlying themes of the analyses provided in *On Truth*. Elsewhere, too, human happiness and that which hinders it constitute a privileged topic for Antiphon. In a late source we find a curious anecdote, which makes him a forerunner of psychoanalysis:

> he invented an art of eliminating pain, just as there is a kind of treatment provided by doctors for people who are sick. In Corinth he established an office next to the

[9] Hobbs 2000: 137–74.

[10] See Kerferd 1981a: 123.

marketplace and advertised that he was able to treat grief-stricken people by means of his speeches. And he inquired into the causes and thereby consoled those people who were suffering. But then, considering that this art was beneath him, he turned to rhetoric.

(87A6 D.-K. = 37P10 L.-M.)[11]

Regrettably, no traces of this art survive; however, the extant fragments of another text, entitled *On Concord* can help clarify his thoughts on the matter, when read alongside *On Truth*.

Certainly, the advice and suggestions that Antiphon used to give his patients were not based on blithe optimism. On the contrary, the dominant tone of the fragments is that of a disenchanted pessimism, typical of much of the Greek gnomic tradition:

Living is like a day-long sentry duty, and the whole length of life is like a single day, as it were, during which no sooner have we raised our eyes toward the light than we pass on the baton to other people who come after us. (87B50 D.-K. = 37D51 L.-M.)

It is astonishingly easy to find fault with all of life, my friend, since it possesses nothing exceptional nor great and imposing, but everything in it is little, weak, ephemeral, and mixed with great pains (87B51 D.-K. = 37D50 L.-M.)

At first sight, these bitter descriptions of human life might seem like yet another variation on the classic theme of human unhappiness, which Antiphon presents through brilliant and evocative images. Upon closer inspection, however, some original insights emerge. In particular, it is worth noting that the undeniable pessimism of the fragments is constantly associated with the theme of intelligence: according to Antiphon, the true cause of distress, in general, is not the wretchedness of the human condition, but the poor use to which people put their intelligence, making things even more difficult instead of solving their problems.[12] Life is complicated and the choices we have to make – when it comes to things such as marriages, children, money, and friendship (87B49, 53–8 D.-K. = 37D57, 52–3, 59, 47a–b, 54–5 L.-M.) – are difficult ones. Unfortunately, instead of using their intelligence to deal with these thorny problems, humans often allow themselves to be driven by impulses and passions to commit acts they will soon regret, but which

[11] Cf. also 87A6 D.-K. (= 37P9 L.-M.): 'When Antiphon had attained a great degree of persuasive power and was nicknamed "Nestor" because he could succeed in persuading people when he spoke about anything, he announced that he would give lectures capable of eliminating pain, as he supposed that no one could name to him a grief so terrible that he could not banish it from that man's thought.'

[12] Gagarin 2002: 95.

cannot be erased, since 'it is not possible to retract one's life like a move in checkers' (87B52 D.-K. = 37D48 L.-M.); and 'the time that they are neglecting is gone' (87B53a D.-K. = 37D53 L.-M.).

What is most striking about Antiphon's distress is the lack of any moralistic overtones and the lucid realism of his observations. Take the example of wealth, a conventional good whose importance Antiphon does not wish to dispute, and which constitutes a recurrent theme in surviving testimonies (87A3, B53–4 D.-K. = 37D83, 52, 59 L.-M.).[13] It is difficult to deny the importance of wealth, and this view had been memorably expressed by Aristodemus, one of the seven wise men: 'Surely no witless word was this of the Spartan, I deem, "Wealth is the worth of a man (*chremat' aner*); a poverty void of esteem"' (Alceus, fr. 49 Lobel-Page = D.L. 1.31). Whether we like it or not, wealth is not something that can be ignored: to reject it completely, as though it served no purpose, is to adopt a fruitless position that is of little use in everyday life. Instead, we should address various concrete questions: if wealth marks the social value of a person, we should also be concerned to ensure that it is acquired in an honest and correct way; in turn, the problem of the acquisition of wealth requires us to more deeply investigate its actual management, preservation, increase, circulation, and so on – and these spawned the first 'economic' reflections. These are only some of the problems that Antiphon dealt with, favouring the 'mercantilistic' view – a minority view at the time – according to which the circulation of money was a legitimate way to gain wealth, in opposition both to the traditional practice of saving money and to those philosophers who merely criticized wealth, without making any significant contributions to the debate (Xenophon informs us of a polemic of Antiphon against Socrates on the matter, although it is difficult to tell just how reliable this testimony is from a historical perspective[14]). Wealth was a concrete problem for which Antiphon suggests concrete solutions, capable of making life' more free and pleasant' (Xenophon, *Memorabilia*, 1.6 = 87A3.3 D.-K. = 37D83.3 L.-M.). It is easy to imagine that he may have formulated similar arguments concerning other everyday problems, from marriage to work and friendship.

[13] Predictably, given the importance of the problem for an expanding society such as fifth-century Athens, Antiphon was not the only sophist to deal with the issue of wealth: see Gorgias 82B20 D.-K. (= 32D40 L.-M.), Prodicus 84B8–9 D.-K. (=34R4 andP6 L.-M.), and Anon. Iambl. 89.7.1 and 7.8 (40.7.1 and 8 L.-M.); see too Soverini 1998: 45–65 and 81–9; Demont 1993; Bonazzi 2009a: 28–31 and 2016; Gavray 2016.

[14] See Bonazzi 2009a.

With respect to these concrete analyses, what makes Antiphon's position even more interesting is his underlying psychological conception. According to him, there are essentially two driving forces in human life: reason and desire. The problem is to strike a balance between the two.[15] Instead of generally censuring the predominance of desire, an obvious or even trivial fact, we are to employ reason to fulfil those desires and needs that are truly useful, so that they may contribute to our happiness. Within this context we can grasp the importance of two key concepts for Antiphon, *sophrosyne* (temperance) and *homonoia* (concord). Temperance is the intelligence with which in each case we face or fulfil our desires, so as to obtain what can truly bring us pleasure or profit:

> One would attribute temperance (*sophrosyne*) most correctly only to that man who blocks himself from the immediate pleasures of his desire and is himself capable of dominating and defeating himself. But someone who wants to satisfy his desire immediately wants what is worse instead of what is better. (87B58 D.-K. = 37D55 L.-M.)
>
> Someone who has not desired nor touched what is shameful or evil is not temperate (*sophron*): for there is nothing in which he shows himself to be well-ordered by dominating it.
>
> (87B59 D.-K. = 37D56 L.-M.)

The outcome of all this is concord, the inner balance that can be created between the different driving forces of reason and desire that guide human actions (see, for example, 87B44a D.-K. = 37R7 L.-M., whose attribution to Antiphon, however, is uncertain). Moreover, this concord is the precondition for the enjoyment of genuine pleasure (or at any rate for the avoidance of pain): Antiphon's pessimism does not rule hedonism out, but rather leads to it.[16]

Just as in *On Truth*, in *On Concord* Antiphon's privileged object of reflection would appear to be the single individual, who is different from the 'citizen' of the *polis* or from the abstract 'human being' of which philosophers all too often speak. Ultimately, the argument expounded in *On Concord* seems to offer a positive counterpart to the analyses of *On Truth*: Antiphon offers what we might describe as an ethical solution to political problems, which is consistent with his emphasis on the priority of the individual over the community (without ever forgetting, however, that the distinction between ethics and politics had not yet been systematized in the sophists' day). As we have seen, *On*

[15] Bonazzi 2006b.

[16] Capra 1997: 298–303.

Truth had dispelled the illusion that *nomos* can solve the problems which *physis* poses to individuals; for its part, *On Concord* shows that only the individual can find a solution to their problems, to the extent that they succeeds in striking a balance with themselves and with their own needs and desires. In other words, by contrast to the positive assessment of the social and collective dimension of human experience, Antiphon focuses on the limits of coexistence and finds a way out, not in the existence of shared rules, but in the individual's capacity to face life's concrete problems in such a way as to derive the greatest benefit and enjoyment. In opposition to the exterior consensus of *nomos*, Antiphon thus invokes inner concord, which does not require any legal approval in order to remain in force and which each person can establish within him- or herself, by making intelligence prevail over the destructive impulses of the passions. Through moderation and temperance it is possible to restore the right balance with ourselves and with the things that surround us: it is not the laws that ensure security and happiness, but intelligence and the use that people make of it.[17]

Undoubtedly, Antiphon's fragments contain none of the sort of revolutionary truths expounded by those figures who sought to overthrow the whole system of values of their community (let us think of Callicles); but nor do they simply pander to widespread prejudices of the sort that guide many people's actions. Rather, we might speak here of an intention to provoke, designed to drive people to become

[17] Although it chiefly applies to ethical issues, it cannot be ruled out that this 'morality of concord' also had more explicitly political consequences (Bonazzi 2006a). 'Concord' is one of the central terms in the heated ideological and political debate that raged in the years of the Peloponnesian War, so much so that it became one of the key terms that moderates and oligarchs invoked against democratic *nomos*. Likewise, for Antiphon the concept of 'concord' does not amount to a generic call to collective reconciliation, but rather serves to trace the profile of true wise men, who alone ought to govern, since 'nothing is worse for human beings than lack of rules (*anarchias*)' (87B61 D.-K. = 37D63 L.-M.). Concord, then, emerges as the capacity to take care of oneself and others by curbing violent and irrational impulses. Obviously, a thesis of this sort potentially applies to all people, but it is easy to see how the concept could be exploited by the oligarchic faction as a powerful way to criticize the alleged freedom of the democrats: according to oligarchic propaganda – as illustrated by the anonymous author of the *Constitution of the Athenians* – democracy is a system which justifies the unruliness of the masses, which allows the masses to yearn for and achieve more and more, thereby laying the ground for the outbreak of increasingly violent conflicts. When set in its context, this praise of self-control and privileging of intelligence over law lose much of their apparently generic quality and prove closely reminiscent of the typically aristocratic themes that characterize pro-Spartan polemics. Regrettably, the limited number of surviving fragments of *On Concord* do not allow us to further investigate this hypothesis. Be that as it may, the fact that considerations of this sort could be exploited for political and especially anti-democratic purposes is confirmed by the theses of another opponent of (democratic) *nomos*, the oligarch Critias: see e.g. H. Patzer 1974 and Bonazzi 2018: 33–41.

more aware of what they are and of what they do, so as to assign priority to what truly matters: the exercising of one's own intelligence, since 'thought (*gnome*) leads the body, for all humans, toward health and disease and toward everything else' (87B2 D.-K. = 37D1b L.-M.). When it comes to the issue of happiness, therefore, Antiphon once again proves himself to be a subtle thinker who exemplifies what is arguably the most distinctive and interesting aspect of sophistry, namely its capacity to rethink the foundations and assumptions of the Greek tradition, through a subtle dialectic of correction and transformation.

Prodicus' (and Hippias') choice

In an article published in 1930, the great historian of antiquity Arnaldo Momigliano developed an intriguing interpretation of Prodicus, in marked opposition to the relativism dominant in the 'ranks of the Thrasymachuses and Callicleses'. At least on the ethical level, unlike in the case of the debate on the origin of the gods (see Chapter 6), Prodicus appears to have aligned himself with traditional morality, defending the need for strong moral principles in everyday life. To support his reconstruction, Momigliano relied on two elements, the predominantly ethical focus of Prodicus' research on language, and especially his famous apologue *The Choice of Heracles*, reported by Xenophon.[18] One noteworthy aspect of Prodicus' almost obsessive interest in linguistic distinctions concerned ethical terms, and in particular the distinction between terms with positive and negative meanings: this might suggest that one of the primary aims of his research was to curb the linguistic conventionalism common in his day, and the practical relativism stemming from it.[19] Moreover, the idea that the defence of

[18] Xenophon, *Memorabilia*, 2.1.21–34 (= 84B2 D.-K. = 34D21 L.-M.). Recently, Dorion 2008 has denied that the passage from Xenophon is a reliable testimony on Prodicus, arguing that the apologue is used to investigate ethical issues addressed by Xenophon's Socrates. This is an intriguing hypothesis, which highlights some interesting affinities between Socrates and Prodicus, but which fails in its attempt to disprove Prodicus' authorship. Certainly, this text is not to be taken as a word-by-word quotation (as suggested instead by Sansone 2004, criticized by Gray 2006); rather, in the light of the introductory expressions used by Xenophon, it is more reasonable to assume that what we have is a summary of Prodicus' argument: see now Mayhew 2011: 201–21.

[19] Momigliano 1930: 102–3. The frequency of ethical terms among Prodicus' synonyms has also been noted by many other scholars: see esp. De Romilly 1986, Dumont 1986, Tordesillas 2004, and Wolfsdorf 2008a. However, in many cases it is difficult to establish whether we are dealing with reliable testimonies (as in the case of 84A19 D.-K. = 34D6a L.-M.) or mere parodies (as is probably the case with 84A15 D.-K. = 34D22 and 23–5 L.-M.). A testimony by Galen (84B4

traditional morality was one of the cornerstones of Prodicus' reflection would appear to find eloquent confirmation in *The Choice of Heracles*, whose edifying tone was widely appreciated even by readers usually hostile to the sophists' teaching, such as Xenophon himself.

It seems as though Prodicus' case was not an isolated one. Broadening our enquiry, we might find an interesting parallel in Hippias' *Trojan Discourse* (86B5 D.-K. = 36D5 L.-M.), which is another example of what a public declamation by a sophist probably sounded like, and which seems to share the same aims as *The Choice of Heracles*. As far as we can tell, the underlying topic of the two speeches is the same: to provide moral advice to young people who are entering adulthood and hence are about to join the true life of the *polis*. Prodicus relates that Heracles was considering what conduct to adopt in his life, when he met two female figures. The first woman, who is called Happiness by her friends and Vice by her detractors, wore flashy clothes and make-up, and immediately stepped forward to promise the hero a life of pleasure. The second woman, Virtue, was instead sober and discrete, and promised the young hero toil but also fame and glory. Although this is not explicitly stated in the text, it is easy to infer that Heracles chose the second woman, who promised to make a model citizen and man of him. Regrettably, Hippias' *Trojan Discourse* has not been preserved, yet in antiquity it was no less famous than *The Choice of Heracles*: against the background of the siege of Troy, the wise Nestor gives young Neoptolemus some practical advice on how to achieve fame and success. It seems as though both texts presented the kind of arguments that might have pleased parents who were concerned about their sons' future. Hippias' position could be compared to Prodicus' and his defence of the need for strong moral principles in everyday life, in opposition to the more radical theses developed by other sophists. Hence, what emerges is a rather clear-cut rift between the various sophists on the issue of virtue and happiness.

This reconstruction, which is not an implausible one, once again confirms that we cannot regard the sophists as exponents of a compact and homogeneous movement. However, a closer inspection of the available sources also suggests that we should avoid drawing sharp contrasts and tone down the opposition between subversive and egoistic

D.-K. = 34D9 L.-M.), concerning *phlegma* (inflammation), shows that Prodicus was not exclusively interested in ethical terms.

sophists on the one hand and sophists open to tradition on the other. We have already noted how immoralism resulted more from a negative interpretation of their views by their detractors (Aristophanes, Plato, and others) than a position which was actually upheld by the sophists. It is a matter now of reassessing Prodicus' and Hippias' theses with respect to traditional knowledge and values, and of verifying that some apparent banalities[20] conceal interesting insights, which can be fruitfully compared with what has been noted with regard to other sophists. The freedom and heterogeneity of the sophists does not exclude a range of common interests and ideas.

Given the almost complete absence of any information on Hippias' discourse, we should focus our attention on Prodicus. Undoubtedly, his discourse complied with the civic ideology that assigned glory to those who had committed themselves to the public good, resisting the temptation of immediate gratification (84B2.28 D.-K. = 34D21.28 L.-M.). Still, we must be careful to avoid drawing a clear-cut contrast between pleasure and virtue, as though these were two incompatible concepts. Prodicus' aim is not to teach contempt for pleasure and encourage the virtues of toil and hard work, but rather to show that true pleasure, the kind of enjoyment which can accompany a person throughout their life, often stands in opposition to immediate gratification, which can soon turn into pain and affliction. It is not a matter, then, of drawing a contrast between pleasure and hard work, but of knowing what is truly good and hence what really brings pleasure and happiness:

> A life entirely focused on eating before being hungry, on sleeping...because one has nothing to do, on pursuing sexual enjoyment without feeling any sexual urge or need is certainly not a pleasant life. What Virtue champions, then, is not the negation or condemnation of pleasure: it is not a matter of seeking out pleasures in themselves...but, on the contrary, of only indulging in them when this means meeting the vital needs of man, for only then do they truly bring enjoyment.[21]

In addition to this, we must bear in mind the utilitarian and individualistic perspective on which the whole discourse is based. The choice of leading a virtuous and noble life is not an end in itself; rather, it is made because of the advantages it brings: Prodicus does not invite us to

[20] Guthrie 1971: 277–8.

[21] Casertano 2004: 78. Some very interesting observations on this hedonistic perspective may be found in Capra 1997: 289–98.

sacrifice ourselves for the public good, but shows that, ultimately, a life of commitment will prove more enjoyable and convenient; and it is for this reason, on account of its usefulness, that it is preferable.[22] No doubt, in his exhortations Prodicus does not oppose traditional morality, but rather draws upon many of its ideas (cf. Hesiod, *Works and Days*, 286–97; Simonides, fr. 386 Page). But this does not imply a clear break with respect to the other sophists: Prodicus' emphasis on personal advantage and the centrality of the individual, just like his interest in the issue of pleasure, is undoubtedly reminiscent of Antiphon.[23] In other words, like Antiphon, Prodicus would appear to adopt a nuanced stance with respect to traditional morality, which is not rejected (he does not deny the importance of honour, just as Antiphon does not deny the importance of wealth) but is rather reassessed according to a different hierarchy of values (where the individual comes before the community).

To further clarify the complexity of Prodicus' approach to tradition, we should not overlook the self-promotional tone of his discourse: the purpose of a discourse, of a public *epideixis*, is not simply to convey an argument but to advertise a teacher.[24] Significantly, the distinctive feature of the discourse, as it has reached us, is not so much the fact that Heracles chooses the path of virtue as the fact that he does so after debating two opposing theses.[25] In such a way, the discourse implicitly yet quite clearly opposes the traditional conception of education, which was often seen as consisting in the passive learning of precepts and norms of conduct: on the contrary, true education must prepare us for making distinctions and assessments. This, in turn, highlights the central importance of the teacher, who alone can teach us how to reason and argue correctly. Heracles was an ambiguous figure, known for having rid the world of monsters (Pindar, *Nemean* 3) but also for yielding to anger, desire, and pleasure (consider, for instance, Euripides' *Alcestis*, Sophocles' *Women of Trachis*, and Aristophanes' *Frogs*). This makes him the ideal pupil for a sophist, and Prodicus can portray

[22] In this respect, it has been observed that the criterion of usefulness appears to have played a part even in the case of linguistic distinctions: in other words, it is reasonable to suggest that the primary aim of the distinction drawn between positive and negative terms was to identify what course of action one ought to follow. See Dumont 1986 and Tordesillas 2004: 61–3. Notwithstanding the reservations expressed in n. 19 above, this is an intriguing hypothesis.

[23] Significantly, Prodicus would appear to share Antiphon's dualist psychology, if De Romilly 1986: 6 is correct in noting that his linguistic distinctions are always based on a contrast between terms associated with the spheres of irrationality and rationality.

[24] See the crucial analysis provided by Morgan 2000: 106–15.

[25] Dorion 2009b: 536 n. 34.

himself as the perfect teacher, whose merit lies not in his conformity to traditional values (something expected in public performance), but in his capacity to teach one how to put forward reasons for each matter at issue and adequately assess them. Once again, what distinguishes the sophists' discourse is its dynamic relation with tradition, which combines the borrowing of certain ideas and a degree of conformity (Heracles ultimately chooses virtue) with certain changes. This is all the more true given that the tale of Heracles at the crossroads was invented by Prodicus himself, who thereby adapted myth to suit his own educational purposes.[26]

The same kind of tension is also to be found in Hippias' *Trojan Discourse* (86B5 D.-K. = 36D5 L.-M.), where the protagonist's choice is even more indicative of the provocative character of the sophists' message. Whereas Heracles remained an ambiguous figure, Neoptolemus was an infamous one, insofar as during the siege of Troy he had killed the elderly Priam, who had taken refuge at the altar of Zeus. The dramatic context of Hippias' speech is therefore highly revealing, because it is precisely after the seizing of Troy, which is to say just after Neoptolemus' terrible crime, that Nestor addresses words of advice to the young man. Neoptolemus' case is even more problematic than that of Heracles, but it is also better suited to the world of the second half of the fifth century, a world that was experiencing a dramatic war and crisis; and Hippias, like a new Nestor capable not only of educating the young but of leading them to success, can present himself as an ideal master for these tumultuous times.[27] Like Prodicus, he applies a subtle strategy of appropriation of tradition and its values: he does not criticize its assumptions or principles, but exploits them for his own purposes. If we think of the way in which Protagoras and Gorgias had engaged with poetic lore (see Chapter 3), here too the divergence from the other sophists turns out to be less marked than what at first appeared to be the case. All sophists, each in his own way, present themselves as masters of virtue; and this is why Plato criticized them so harshly, in the belief that their teaching, far from leading one to the true good, only exacerbated the defects of traditional morality.

[26] Kuntz 1993.

[27] In this respect, it is interesting to note that, in the *Protagoras*, Plato parodies Hippias in the figure of Nestor: see Brancacci 2004. Nestor is certainly a paradigmatic figure, also apparently evoked by Gorgias (82B14 D.-K. = 32D52 L.-M.) and Antiphon (87A6 D.-K. = 37P9 L.-M.).

VI THE GODS AND RELIGION

The theme of the gods, of their existence, appearance, and interest in human affairs, was an object of constant attention for the Greeks from the most ancient times. As is widely known, Greek religion presents some highly original features compared with present-day religions: there are no religious texts establishing a body of orthodox doctrines, and no figures to whom worship is officially entrusted. Perhaps precisely because of this fluid situation, the element of the divine marks almost all salient moments in the lives of individuals and cities.[1] This constant presence in itself explains why, from Homer onwards, all writers were so keen to explore the issue of the gods. In particular, many Presocratic philosophers staunchly criticized popular prejudices (often presenting the gods as thieves, adulterers, and seducers) by suggesting alternative and more rigorous conceptions. In doing so, the Presocratics changed the content of the divine, without denying its existence:[2] they opposed the theology of the philosophers to the theology of the poets. The sophists also fit within this broader movement towards the critical redefinition of traditional religiosity, a movement which engaged many leading personalities of the age: let us think of Euripides, of Thucydides' analysis of the plague, or of the debate on the 'sacred disease' (epilepsy) among Hippocratic doctors. In particular, the sophists stand out on account of what we might term their 'sociological' perspective: while criticizing the phenomenon of religion, they acknowledged its importance in human life; searching for its causes, they embarked on enquiries into the nature of the gods, the origin of the belief in their existence, their role in people's lives, and myths as a means to convey traditional values.

The outcomes of these enquiries are often provocative, to the point that (in some cases, at least) they border on atheism, a multifaceted concept:[3] some sophists are included in the lists of atheists that circulated in the Hellenistic and Imperial centuries.[4] This partly

[1] Muir 1985:193–5.

[2] Kahn 1997: 250–3.

[3] In the ancient world, the term 'atheist' did not only describe someone who denies the existence of the gods, but also someone who scorns the gods or has been abandoned by them (see Winiarczyk 1990). In the following pages, the term will mostly be used in its modern sense. In general on ancient atheism, see now Sedley 2013, Whitmarsh 2015, and Gourinat 2019.

[4] Usually these lists included the names of Prodicus, Diagoras, Critias, Theodore of Cyrene, Euhemerus of Messene, and – with some reservations – Protagoras: see Gigon 1985: 423.

explains the violent reactions to their teachings in Athens. Given the freedom with which the problem of the divine was investigated from the most ancient times, one might have expected to find a certain degree of tolerance towards debates and criticism even in the fifth century.[5] Instead, the opposite was the case, especially in the second half of the century, when war raged between Athens and Sparta. While Dodds may have gone too far in describing this as a period of resurgent irrationalism, excesses occurred in both directions.[6] Probably in 437 BC, Diopeithes' decree was issued to denounce those who did not believe in the existence of the gods or spoke on celestial matters (*ta meteora*).[7] On the opposite side of the spectrum, we know that, a few years later, a club of *kakodaimonists* ('companions of the evil daemon') was founded, whose members would meet to enjoy a banquet on what were regarded as unlucky days. Finally, we have the case of the Hermocopids (those who smashed the Hermes statues in Athenian streets) and the profanation of the Mysteries in 415 BC. Within this context, it appears that many representatives of the new culture were brought to trial.[8] Then, of course, we have the most famous trial of all: we should not forget that one of the two charges in the trial which led to Socrates' death was that the philosopher did not respect the traditional gods and had introduced new deities. The sophists appear to have been both a symptom and a cause of this climate of unrest.[9] Much of their fame, and of the hatred they attracted, depends precisely on their provocations in this field.

Protagoras' agnosticism

Protagoras' penchant for sensational statements, capable of seizing the public's attention, is further confirmed by the opening of another text by him, probably entitled *On the Gods*:[10]

[5] Betegh 2006: 625.

[6] Dodds 1951: 188–95.

[7] The authenticity of this decree has been repeatedly disputed; a recent defence of its historicity is in Whitmarsh 2015: 117–19.

[8] Trials have been recorded for Anaxagoras, Diagoras, Protagoras, Prodicus, Euripides, Phidias, and Aspasia. However, in particular with regard to Protagoras and Prodicus, it seems that the sources are not always reliable: see the overview provided by Ostwald 1986: 528–36, and Bonazzi 2018: 43–7.

[9] Burkert 1985a: 311–17.

[10] At present, it is still difficult to establish the relation between this text and the *Truth*. What is more interesting to note is that the sources also credit Protagoras with a treatise *On What Is in Hades* (80A1 D.-K. = 31D1 L.-M.), which would appear to confirm his interest in the topic.

About the gods I am able to know neither that they exist nor that they do not exist nor of what kind they are in form: for many things prevent me for knowing this, its obscurity and the brevity of man's life. (80B4 D.-K. = 31D10 L.-M.)[11]

According to one ancient tradition this statement had a disproportionate effect, far beyond what the sophist could imagine: 'because of the beginning of his book [i.e. *On the Gods*], Protagoras was expelled by the Athenians, and they burned his books in the marketplace after they had been collected by a herald from everyone who owned them' (80A1 D.-K. = 31P19); and 'while he was travelling from the mainland to the islands and avoiding Athenian triremes, which were deployed on all the seas, he suffered shipwreck while sailing a small boat' (80A2 D.-K. = 31P21 L.-M.). According to Philostratus, the source of the second quote, Protagoras' impiety was due to his Persian education – as though it were impossible for a Greek to come up with such ideas.[12]

Be that as it may, the sophist was made the object of unanimous and enduring condemnation, to the point of bringing together traditionally antithetical schools of thought, such as the Christians and the Epicureans: Protagoras of Abdera, the son of Manander, stated that neither gods nor God exist at all (Epiphanius, *Against Heresies*, 3.16), and

Protagoras of Abdera in effect maintained the same opinion as Diagoras, but he used different words on the idea that he would thereby avoid its excessive temerity. For he said that he did not know whether the gods exist. But this is the same as saying that one knows that they do not exist. (Diogenes of Oenoanda, 80A23 D.-K. = 31R24 L.-M.)

However, the anecdotes we have regarding Protagoras' life are probably false,[13] and there is no reason to assume a profession of atheism on his part:

Diogenes crassly conflates a profession of knowledge ('I know that not-*P*') with a confession of ignorance ('I do not know that *P*'). To the believer, agnostics may be as bad as atheists; but to the atheists agnostics are not much better than believers.[14]

For a recent and very detailed analysis of this fragment, see Corradi 2017 with further bibliography.

[11] On the text, see Di Benedetto 2001.

[12] On Protagoras and the Magi, see Gigon 1985: 427–30.

[13] See Corradi 2012: 31–43.

[14] Barnes 1979: ii.449–50.

In other words, this is not an ontological thesis but an epistemological one:[15] Protagoras is the first thinker to take an agnostic stance, which can hardly be understood as an expression of atheism.

But while it is evident that Protagoras' statement is not a profession of atheism, its overall meaning is less clear. Some interpreters have even gone so far as to deny that he is doubting the existence of the gods in this passage. This position has been endorsed in particular by Kerferd, who has established a parallel between the use of *hos* in this statement and in the 'man-measure' one: in the latter case, as we have seen, the preposition clearly has a modal meaning (see pp. 17–18); if we assume that it was used in the same sense in the former passage, we must conclude that Protagoras was chiefly interested in the way in which the gods are and present themselves, rather than in their presumed existence or non-existence. He would thus be claiming that we do not know 'how' the gods are or are not, and the words that follow ('nor of what kind they are in form') would have an almost epexegetic function (or would more concretely refer to the problem of their visible appearance[16]). This would imply, then, that Protagoras never raised any doubts as to the existence of the gods. Against this reading, however, it must be noted that all the ancient sources, from Plato onwards (see *Theaetetus*, 162d), unanimously present Protagoras' thesis as though it concerned the existence of the gods. As there are no reasons to go against such a solid tradition, the most reasonable hypothesis is that the passage discussed both the existence of the gods ('neither that they exist nor that they do not exist') and their form ('nor of what kind they are in form'[17]). Incidentally, it is worth noting that the statement possibly presents the first recorded use of the verb 'to be' in an existential sense.[18]

The reasons which Protagoras reportedly adduced in support of his thesis – the obscurity of the problem and the brevity of human life – have been regarded as too banal, or at any rate not particularly relevant.[19] However, they acquire greater significance when viewed in relation to a concept the importance of which has already been stressed in relation to the 'man-measure', namely personal experience: this is

[15] Drozdek 2005: 41.
[16] See Kerferd 1981a: 165–9.
[17] See Di Benedetto 2001.
[18] Kahn 1973: 302.
[19] Barnes 1979: ii.450.

the only legitimate criterion to verify our knowledge.[20] Therefore it seems that, by highlighting the limits of human experience, Protagoras was engaging in a polemic with those Presocratic thinkers, such as Parmenides and Empedocles, who had repeatedly claimed to be able to transcend the limits of human knowledge, as well as the poets, who had based their authority on a privileged contact with the divine world. In this respect, some interesting similarities are to be found between Protagoras and the sixth-century poet and moralist Xenophanes of Elea (21B34 D.-K. = 8D49 L.-M.), who also reportedly criticized human claims to know the truth about the gods (significantly, for Xenophanes too, obscurity is an obstacle to knowledge).[21] The analogies with Xenophanes become even more striking when we consider the second segment of the first statement, concerning the presumed appearance of the gods. In raising this problem, Protagoras was in all likelihood referring to the anthropomorphic conception, which Xenophanes had already repeatedly censured.[22] And in doing so, Xenophanes had not been alone either, because we can also add Herodotus' words:[23] 'what appearance the gods have' is something which Homer and Hesiod had established for the Greeks, but it was only a poetic fiction (Herodotus 2.53.1). The polemic does not concern only the Presocratics but also, and most importantly, traditional forms of religious expression.

One intriguing problem for scholars has been to reconstruct the follow-up to this text. It is difficult to imagine that, after a statement of this sort, Protagoras continued to speak at length about the gods. The structure of the sentence (and in particular the presence of the particle *men*, which implies a contrasting *de*) suggests that the author shifted his attention onto human beings: for the Greeks, the notions of god and human were mutually defining.[24] As Werner Jaeger has suggested, it is likely that, in the continuation of the text, Protagoras

[20] Mansfeld 1981: 41–2.

[21] It is interesting to note that a statement similar to Protagoras' has been attributed to Parmenides' pupil Melissus, who was a polemical target of the sophists: 'He said that we ought not to make any statements about the gods, for it was impossible to have knowledge of them' (D.L. 9.24).

[22] Sassi 2013; see also Corradi 2017: 456–61. Alternatively, Protagoras may have been referring to the repeated transformations of the gods in Greek myths: this too militated against the possibility of saying anything definite about their form (Drozdek 2005: 42).

[23] On the relation between this passage from Herodotus and Protagoras, see Burkert 1985b, who has emphasized the dependence of the former on the latter, and the words of caution voiced by Sassi 2013.

[24] Mansfeld 1981: 43.

discussed not the problem of the gods in itself, but rather the issue of what they represent for human beings, thereby inaugurating an anthropological and sociological approach that considers religion in terms of its function for human civilization and society.[25] This is no doubt a noteworthy suggestion. What is less convincing is the way in which this hypothesis has been developed. From Jaeger onwards, scholars have believed that, while leaving the problem of the actual existence of the gods open, Protagoras celebrated their importance for human civilization.[26] Given the silence of fragment B4, this hypothesis is based on the myth that Protagoras relates in the dialogue named after him. Yet, even leaving aside the problem of the Protagorean origin of this page of Plato's (a far from trivial problem[27]), what may be inferred from the myth is in fact the very opposite. In the myth, Protagoras acknowledges the importance of belief in the gods as something specifically and universally human; but the very moment that he acknowledges the presence of the religious dimension, he de facto limits its importance by implying that this belief (or fear) is not enough to provide a foundation for human society. What ensures that people can live together in cities is rather politics, which is the object of the sophists' teaching. Protagoras' agnosticism is therefore instrumental for his radical humanism.[28]

The origin of the belief in the gods

As far as we can tell, Prodicus investigated not so much the problem of the gods themselves as the origins of the human belief in their existence (84B5 D.-K. = 34D15–18 L.-M.). In all likelihood, in this respect too it was Prodicus' interest in names, a distinguishing feature of his activity as a sophist, that conditioned his reflections. According to his

[25] Jaeger 1947: 176. See also Corradi 2012: 169–70, on the basis of Plato, *Cratylus*, 400d–401a.

[26] In addition to Jaeger, consider for instance Schiappa 1991, pp. 141–148 or, more recently, Drozdek 2005.

[27] See Bonazzi 2011.

[28] As further confirmation of this humanism, one might recall the ideas on crime and punishment that Plato puts into Protagoras' mouth in the dialogue named after him (*Prot.* 323c–324d; however, it is difficult to establish whether these are ideas that may historically be traced back to Protagoras: see Saunders 1981). The underlying thesis – that a just punishment must not be a reprisal, but must rather serve as a means of correction and deterrent – stands out insofar as it aims to investigate the problem of injustice and evil among human beings without invoking, or confiding in, any corrective action on the gods' part.

perspective, the gods are a human product, insofar as people have chosen to regard as 'divine' that which has proven useful to their lives: at first, things such as the sun and moon, rivers and fruits; later, 'as human wit entered into competition with nature',[29] this was also extended to those people who had distinguished themselves with inventions that were particularly useful for the well-being of humanity.[30] According to Henrichs' reconstruction, a transition was essentially made from an impersonal stage, in which beneficial objects were deified (e.g. bread or wine), to a personal stage, in which the object of deification were those people to whom the invention could be attributed, or who at any rate had taught others how to correctly employ useful things (as in the case of Demeter and Dionysus[31]). The gods and religion, then, are merely a human product resulting from humans' attempt to make sense of the environment in which they live.[32] Undoubtedly, the boldness of these ideas, which 'make the gods come down from their pedestal';[33] the parallel reassessment of the human world, which is capable of making sense of reality; and the emphasis on usefulness as the distinguishing criterion to understand and guide one's actions make this theory a typical testimony to the sophists' way of reasoning.

Not unlike in Protagoras' case, the limited number of testimonies we have prevents us from precisely reconstructing the context of Prodicus' theories on the matter. It cannot be ruled out that somehow – and, once again, as in Protagoras' case – this discussion concerning the gods constituted a prelude to an analysis of human civilization.[34] Yet, as far as we can infer from a passage by Themistius (a rhetor from the age of Imperial Rome: 84B5 D.-K. = 34D17 L.-M.), Prodicus would appear to have stressed the importance of agriculture rather than politics, as Protagoras did in the Platonic dialogue. It might be hypothesized, therefore, that

[29] Henrichs 1975: 111.

[30] Guthrie 1971: 238–42 voiced some reservations with regard to the two-phase reconstruction of Prodicus' theory (which entails first the deification of inanimate objects and then that of particularly distinguished human beings), by arguing that the available sources allow us to attribute to Prodicus only the deification of inanimate objects and not of humans as well (the same view is taken by Gomperz 1912: 113 n. 251). However, an oft-neglected testimony, a papyrus fragment from a treatise *On Piety* by the Epicurean Philodemus (PHerc. 1428 = 84B5 D.-K. = 34D15 L.-M.), has made it possible to cast these reservations aside and to attribute the whole theory to Prodicus: see Henrichs 1975: 112–23; Mayhew 2011: 180–3.

[31] See Untersteiner 1947.

[32] Henrichs 1975: 112.

[33] Dorion 2009a: 348.

[34] Nestle 1936.

Prodicus reconstructed a *Kulturgeschichte* in which the progressive improvement of humankind's living conditions was first of all connected to the progress made in the cultivation of the land; and that particular attention was devoted to the relation between civilization, agriculture, and religion.[35]

In the context of the Greek world, whose calendar and festivities revolved around the key moments in the agricultural year, the link drawn by Prodicus would have been a particularly incisive one.[36]

With some caution, Prodicus' view may be regarded as an expression of atheism.[37] An even more explicit atheistic stance has been recorded in an extensive fragment from a satyr-play entitled *Sisyphus*.[38] This text had long been attributed to Critias, and actually constituted one of the main reasons for including this author among the sophists (88B25 D.-K. = Dram. T63 L.-M.). However, the attribution has been disputed, and the name of Euripides has been suggested instead, based on the fact that in 415 BC the tragedian composed a satyr-play entitled *Sisyphus* to accompany a trilogy consisting of *Alexander*, *Palamedes*, and *Trojan Women*.[39] Whether the author is Critias or Euripides, it is important to avoid the mistake of assuming that these verses express his personal views: the lines are spoken by a mythological

[35] Soverini 1998: 105. Further developing his hypothesis, Nestle 1936 had set these doctrines in relation to the famous testimony on Heracles' choice (see Chapter 5, pp. 106–110): indeed, this argument was featured in a text entitled *Horai* (84B1 D.-K. = 34D19 L.-M.), and it may reasonably be assumed that the term referred to the seasons, and therefore that Prodicus celebrated Heracles as a symbol of the world of farmers as well. According to this view, then, the *Horai* provided a praise of agriculture, a theory on the origin of religion connected to agriculture, and an exhortation to virtue (something necessary for agricultural life), embodied by the figure of Heracles at the crossroads. This hypothesis – an intriguing one, yet difficult to prove – may find some confirmation in the testimonies from Aristophanes (*Clouds*, 360–2, and *Birds*, 690–2 = 84A5 D.-K. = Dram. T22 L.-M.) and Timon (fr. 18 Di Marco). These present Prodicus as a *meteorosophist*, an expert on celestial matters: the reference here would not be to cosmological phenomena, but to atmospheric ones such as rain and wind, which Prodicus claimed to know much about (see Soverini 1998: 90–114). However, it is also worth noting that, while certainly important, the connection with agriculture did not exhaust the richness of the apologue on Heracles, which could equally well apply to the world of the *polis* – indeed, it especially referred to this.

[36] Muir 1985: 204. Besides, Antiphon too is credited with a treatise *On Agriculture* (87B118 D.-K., not in L.-M.), and often the sophists are regarded as experts on celestial matters (*meteora*; see preceding footnote): see e.g. Protagoras 80A11 D.-K. = Dram. T18a and Gorgias 82A17 = 32P35 L.-M.

[37] Henrichs 1976; Willink 1983; Mayhew 2011.

[38] See Kerferd 1981a: 171.

[39] Dihle 1977 is the main champion of this new attribution, which has attracted much consensus: see e.g. Scodel 1980: 124; Ostwald 1986: 281; Kahn 1997. However, we also find some champions of the Critias attribution: see e.g. Centanni 1997: 144–59 (very useful on the other tragedies possibly written by Critias); Bultrighini 1999: 213–50; Scholten 2003: 238–57 and Alvoni 2017.

character – and not a great one either, given the sinister reputation surrounding Sisyphus, the deceiver par excellence.[40] In other words, this long fragment counts as a document that attests to the ideas circulating at the time rather than to any independent theory.[41]

The fragment reconstructs the history of humanity by dividing it into three crucial stages: (1) in its first stage, humankind's life was disorderly and bestial, dominated as it was by brute force (lines 1–4); (2) to remedy the situation, human beings established laws ensuring justice and peace, and yet these laws only partially attained the result that was sought after: while they regulated public actions, underhanded acts of violence continued (5–11); (3) someone, 'a man who was shrewd and wise in his planning' (12), then invented the gods: immortal, omniscient, and omnipotent beings capable of reading human beings' thoughts and of acting upon this knowledge – and fear of the gods finally made city life possible (11–42). What we have here is a first attestation of the theory of religion as an *instrumentum regni*, a theory destined to enjoy great popularity, first in Rome and then in the modern world.

Even though it is impossible to establish any direct links, it is interesting to note that this passage stands in contrast to the theories of Prodicus and Protagoras that I have just discussed. Unlike Prodicus, the author of these verses traces the origin of the belief in the gods back not to usefulness, but to fear.[42] Even more marked is his divergence from Protagoras and democratic ideology. While Protagoras celebrates the superiority of politics (and the *nomos*) over religion precisely because of its capacity to regulate the social life of humans, the very opposite is the case in the *Sisyphus*: it is religion, understood as fear of the gods, which safeguards human life. But the real point of divergence does not concern so much the analysis of society as the anthropological conception which this analysis implies: whereas Protagoras stresses a 'collaborative' anthropology, which underlines the political and social dimension of human life, the *Sisyphus* passage entails a very different kind of anthropology, which emphasizes the irremovable nature of the passions and of the instinct

[40] Sutton 1981.

[41] Kahn 1997: 249–50.

[42] An interesting parallel here is with Democritus, 68A75 D.-K. = Atom. D207 L.-M.; see too Euripides, *Helen*, 743.

to overpower others.[43] One truly experiences here the 'bottomless' depth of human nature.[44]

Providence and divine justice: matters of theodicy

One issue which had always been debated in relation to the gods was what in the modern age came to be referred to as the problem of 'theodicy', which is to say the problem of the justification of divine justice vis-à-vis the existence of evil. Faith in the gods entailed confidence in a corrective action on their part, as had constantly been stressed by the greatest poets, from Hesiod (*Works and Days*, 267–73) and Solon (fr. 1, 25–32 D.) onwards. In the second half of the fifth century BC, the Greeks started voicing more and more doubts, reservations, and objections with regard to the effectiveness of this divine intervention, in some case denying its very existence. As a counterpart to Aeschylus' censuring of those who dared to claim 'that the gods did not deign to concern themselves / with such mortals' (*Agamemnon*, 369–72), it is possible to adduce some verses from Euripides that clearly reflect the anxiety felt by the people of his day: 'if the gods are <sensible>, you, just man that you are, will be rewarded. And if not, why should we toil?' (*Iphigenia in Aulis*, 1034–5). Besides, this was the implicit moral of the *Sisyphus*: 'the truth would be that there are no gods and that no unjust man has anything to fear insofar as he can escape the human guardians of law and order'.[45] Protagoras, too, had dealt with this issue in an original way, by attempting to solve the problem of justice without invoking the gods. It is perfectly reasonable to assume, then, that the sophists contributed to this climate of anxiety through the views they expressed.

Other testimonies confirm this, in addition to the ones already discussed. Consider, for instance, the following statement by Thrasymachus:

[43] Evident affinities are instead to be found with Antiphon: see Chapter 4, pp. 84–89. This sort of polemic becomes even more interesting when we consider the fact that another target might have been Socrates' intellectualism. However, it is difficult to agree with Santoro 1997 that the wise inventor of the gods is to be identified precisely with Socrates (more reasonably, Palumbo 2005 suggests the name of Xenophanes – but, again, it is difficult to draw any definite conclusions).

[44] Nestle 1948. On this, see now Balla 2018.

[45] Burkert 1985a: 315.

'The gods do not notice human affairs: for otherwise they would not have failed to take notice of what is the greatest good for humans, justice. For we see that humans do not practice this' (85B8 D.-K. = 35D17 L.-M.).

Generally speaking, this passage has been used to clear Thrasymachus of the charge of immoralism suggested by the *Republic*: scholars have spoken of the 'cry of sorrowful pessimism', of 'an impassioned denunciation', and of 'bitter disillusionment'.[46] However, these heartfelt verdicts may be making too much of the statement, which lends itself, rather, to a more disenchanted reading.[47] Indeed, the passage neither delivers any denunciation nor betrays any bitterness for the way in which people scorn justice. First of all, it acknowledges some facts: that the gods are indifferent towards human events and that humans, while affirming the importance of justice, do not actually abide by it. This observation thus succeeds in its goal of establishing the conflict between entrenched beliefs and forms of behaviour: for if humans truly believed in the power of the gods, they would respect the 'greater good' of justice. In other words, Thrasymachus sticks to the facts; yet, his observation has a startling outcome. When read in such terms, Thrasymachus' statement would appear to be not so much a cry of anguish against his own times as yet another attestation of the rationalism of the sophists, who often build their theses in opposition to traditionally accepted ones, as 'weaker' arguments prevailing over 'stronger' ones.

Whatever the underlying meaning of Thrasymachus' words, it is evident that they could not be taken as an expression of atheism. Still, atheism remained one possible response to the apparent predominance of injustice in human events. A stance against divine providence has been attributed to Antiphon (87B12 D.-K. = 37D37 and R17). In addition to this, considering that Plato seems to allude to him in Book 10 of the *Laws*, we might infer that, in Antiphon, a mechanistic view of the universe went hand in hand with the denial of the existence of the divine.[48] In antiquity, however, the atheist par excellence was not a sophist but a poet, who may have been influenced by the sophists: Diagoras of

[46] Untersteiner 1954: 325; Romeyer-Dherbey 1985: 77; and Guthrie 1971: 297 respectively.

[47] Bonazzi 2008.

[48] See also Chapter 2, pp. 40–41. Some difficulty, in this case, might be raised by fragment 87B10 D.-K. = 37D9a L.-M. ('that is why he lacks nothing and receive nothing from anyone, but is unlimited and unlacking'), which many scholars believe to be referring to god. Other solutions are possible, however, because the subject might be the cosmos, the intellect, or nature: see the discussion in Pendrick 2002: 256–9.

Melos. Regrettably, not much is known about him, and the little information we have consists of trivial anecdotes which do not really help us to reconstruct his ideas.[49] So it is impossible to establish whether – as hypothesized by Guthrie[50] – Diagoras may be the source of theses of the sort we find in a fragment from Euripides' *Bellerophon*:

> Does someone then say that there are gods in heaven?
> There are not, there are not, if a man will
> Not in folly rely on the old argument.
> Consider it yourselves; do not build your opinion
> On my words. I say that a tyranny
> Kills many men and deprives them of their possessions,
> And breaking oaths destroys cities;
> And doing this they are more happy
> Than those who live each day in pious peace.
> And I know of small cities that honour the gods
> Which obey greater and more impious ones,
> Overcome by the greater number of spears.
>
> (fr. 286 Kannicht)[51]

In this case, the argument is based on the incompatibility between the predominance of evil on the one hand and the existence of an omniscient, omnipotent, and benevolent deity on the other. Now, given that apparently there are no reasons to deny the first point, the most reasonable conclusion would be to deny the latter: hence, the gods do not exist.[52]

One interesting element in Euripides' verses is the allusion to the destruction of 'small cities', something which the Greeks unfortunately became aware of during the years of war between Athens and Sparta. One particularly striking episode was the massacre of Melos, Diagoras' home city, in 415 BC: that this might have been the origin of Diagoras' atheism is an intriguing hypothesis, yet one impossible to verify.[53] Certainly, the Melos episode inspired some memorable

[49] The testimonies were brought together in Winiarczyk 1981 and 2016.

[50] Guthrie 1971: 236; but see now the more detailed treatment in Whitmarsh 2015: 109–13.

[51] Translated Barnes 1979.

[52] See Barnes 1979: ii.455–6 for an analysis of the merits and limitations of this argument.

[53] From the few testimonies we have about Diagoras' life, it seems as though he was charged with impiety and forced to flee Athens precisely in 415/414 BC: see Winiarczyk 2016: 54–59. A scholium to Aristophanes would appear to establish a correlation between his impiety (and in particular his profanation of the Eleusinian Mysteries) and the Melos event (*Scholia in Aristoph. Aves*, 1073); see also Brisson 1994. However, Diagoras' atheism had long been known: see Ostwald 1986: 275–7. As far as Euripides' *Bellerophon* is concerned, it can be dated between 430 and 426 BC.

pages by another great author of the fifth century; once again, this is not a sophist but a writer deeply influenced by the sophists: Thucydides. When introducing the Melos episode in Book 5 of his *History*, Thucydides imagines a dialogue between the Athenian ambassadors and the representatives of Melos to discuss the surrender of the 'small city' to the imperial power of Athens. The structure of what is often referred to as the 'Melian Dialogue', arranged according to opposite theses, clearly reflects the influence of sophistic antilogies, as does the content of the arguments: scholars have, for instance, repeatedly observed that the Athenians defend the same notion of justice as the one that Plato attributes to Thrasymachus in the *Republic*, namely the idea that justice comes from might. By contrast, scholars have often failed to note that the dialogue also includes a most interesting variation on the theme of the divine and of theodicy.

Towards the end of the dispute, when it is clear that any settlement between the two parties is impossible, the Melians openly accuse the Athenians of injustice, while voicing their faith in a providential intervention of the gods (who are expected to somehow force the Spartans – whose colonists the Melians are – to come to their aid):

> Melians: We, too, be well assured, think it difficult to contend both against your power and against fortune, unless she shall be impartial; but nevertheless we trust that, in point of fortune, we shall through the divine favour be at no disadvantage because we are god-fearing men standing our ground against men who are unjust…
>
> Athenians: Well, as to the kindness of the divine favour, neither do we expect to fall short of you therein. For in no respect are we departing from men's observances regarding that which pertains to the divine or from their desires regarding that which pertains to themselves in aught that we demand or do. For of the gods we hold the belief, and of men we know, that by a necessity of their nature wherever they have the power they always rule. And so in our case since we neither enacted this law nor when it was enacted were the first to use it, but found it in existence and expect to leave it in existence for all time, so we make use of it, well aware that both you and others, if clothed with the same power as we are, would do the same thing. And so with regard to the divine favour, we have good reason not to be so afraid that we shall be at a disadvantage.
>
> (Thucydides, 5.104–5)

While one might disagree with the Athenians' words, their originality can hardly be disputed: to defend themselves, they did not simply reject the belief that any providential divine intervention was possible, as Thrasymachus might have done, for instance; neither did they deny the existence of the gods, like the *Bellerophon* or Diagoras; nor yet did they endorse an agnostic stance like Protagoras. On the contrary, the Athenians affirmed their 'piety' by developing a sort of 'negative' theology. The starting point of their reasoning is the opposition between knowledge and opinion, which draws upon the reflections of thinkers such as Protagoras and Xenophanes: certainty only concerns human facts, whereas when it comes to the gods we can only rely on opinions – the kind of opinions which make up the Greek tradition. But what can be inferred from these opinions? What is their teaching? Whether we read Homer or the theogonies, lyric poems or tragedies, the moral is always the same: the gods rule because they are more powerful; and this is the conclusion which we (undoubtedly, in all certainty) reach if we consider human events. Hence, in the light of shared opinions, as well as of the actual behaviour of human beings, the Athenians find confirmation of their thesis: the justice of humans and gods consists in the predominance of those who are stronger; and if justice consists in the exercising of strength, then it must be concluded that the Athenians are those who most faithfully follow the gods, precisely insofar as they impose their own might.[54]

What are we to make, then, of this negative theology? Clearly, we cannot attribute it to Thucydides, nor must we necessarily attribute it to the anonymous Athenians of his text, given that the latter dialectically inferred it from traditional morality. Be that as it may, what we have here is one of the most revealing examples of the way in which many fifth-century authors reasoned, especially the sophists. Its hallmarks are an inquisitiveness and desire to investigate problems to their utmost limits, and a taste for provocation. The historian Gregory Crane has claimed that Thucydides 'writes to shock': the same description perfectly applies to the sophists as well.[55]

[54] Significant similarities may be found in Book 10 of the *Laws*: 'All this, my friends, is the theme of experts – as our young people regard them – who in their prose and poetry maintain that anything one can get away with by force is absolutely justified. This is why we experience outbreaks of impiety among the young, who assume that the kind of gods the laws tell them to believe in do not exist; this is why we get treasonable efforts to convert people to the "true natural life", which is essentially nothing but a life of conquest over others, not one of service to your neighbor as the law enjoins' (Pl. *Leg.* 10.890a–b). On the possible references to Antiphon in this passage, see above and Chapter 2, pp. 40–41. It is interesting to note that in antiquity Antiphon was regarded as one of Thucydides' masters: the hypothesis that these passages from the Melians' dialogue betray the sophist's influence is intriguing, but impossible to demonstrate based on the available testimonies.

[55] Crane 1998: 6.

APPENDIX 1: THE PROTAGONISTS

As already noted in Chapter 1, it is difficult to pinpoint the number and identity of all the sophists who in the fifth century BC travelled from city to city educating Greece, as Hegel put it, or corrupting it, as Aristophanes believed. In what follows, an attempt will be made to provide an exhaustive overview of the most authoritative sophists, without overlooking those minor, or not so well-documented, figures who present some interesting features.[1]

Protagoras of Abdera

In antiquity the life and philosophical career of Protagoras – arguably the most famous sophist – became the object of many, mostly unreliable, stories. We know for certain that he was born in Abdera, Thrace, around 490 BC – the first half of the fifth century. Despite some evidence to the contrary, it is likely that he came from a wealthy family, one which even gave hospitality to Xerxes at the time of the Persian Wars. It is also reported that, in return, Xerxes granted the family the rare privilege of having their son Protagoras educated by the Magi (even if one chooses to regard this story as spurious, it still confirms the contacts between Protagoras and the culture of the Ionian colonies and those of the Near East). Later he travelled around Greece as a teacher, earning great fame and amassing considerable riches. It is equally certain that Protagoras repeatedly sojourned in Athens in the time of Pericles, with whom he established personal ties. It is difficult to tell whether these contacts also led to a direct involvement in the democratic politics of the great statesman. Evidence in this direction is apparently provided not just by the sophist's surviving fragments, but also by the fact that, in 444 BC, Pericles entrusted Protagoras with drafting the constitution of the new pan-Hellenic colony of Thurii in Magna Graecia (clearly, an

[1] In certain cases, these profiles draw and expand upon the introductory notes provided by Bonazzi 2007 (on Protagoras, see too Bonazzi 2009b). Other detailed presentations may be found in Kent Sprague 1972, Kerferd 1981a: 42–58, Guthrie 1971: 261–319, and Pradeau 2009a. With regard to the Platonic figures, Nails 2002 is also very useful. On ancient philosophers more generally, I will refer to Goulet 1989–2018.

appointment of this sort implies that the two men shared the same political views). This connection with Pericles can also be confirmed by the upheavals that marked the last years of Protagoras' life: the crisis of Periclean politics seems to find a counterpart in the downfall of Protagoras, who – like other personalities close to the statesman – was reportedly put on trial.

But the information we have here becomes very hazy. Some sources report that, after a public reading of his text on the gods, Protagoras was charged with impiety and fled Athens, while his books were burned. By the same account, the sophist died in a shipwreck during his flight. However, this is very questionable; in particular, it differs from what Plato writes in his dialogues, where he speaks of Protagoras as though he had died as a universally esteemed figure in old age, with no references to any trials or flights. From Plato we know that Protagoras lived approximately seventy years (other sources state ninety), which would place his death at around 420 BC.

Diogenes Laertius attributes many works to Protagoras, but a comparison with the other sources reveals that his list is incomplete. Worse still, what are missing from Diogenes' list are precisely the most important and controversial works, such as *Truth* and *On the Gods*. One possible explanation is that these two texts constituted individual entries of the *Antilogiae* (*Opposing Arguments*, mentioned by Diogenes), which were possibly also known as *Kataballontes logoi* (*The Overthrower Arguments* or, better, *The Knockdown Arguments*: see Appendix 2). Yet, as in other cases, any attempt at reconstruction is destined to remain a mere hypothesis, given the dearth of available fragments. Indeed, apart from the title of Protagoras' work, all we have are a few authentic fragments and many interpretations. Ever since antiquity, his provocative theses have elicited interest and criticism from his readers. As a result, different reconstructions of his thought are available, which are not always reliable and are often clearly shaped by disparaging intentions.

The first and most important tradition stretches back to Plato, who devoted two dialogues to the theses of the sophist of Abdera, the *Protagoras* and the *Theaetetus*. Many of the later testimonies, starting with Aristotle's, appear to depend on Plato's discussion, and this must be taken into account when examining the information from our sources. Alongside the Platonic tradition, another tradition proved influential in antiquity, namely the one that highlighted the sceptical implications of Protagoras' thought. However, little is known about this interpretation because sceptics such as Sextus Empiricus explicitly refused to be associated with Protagoras, whom they regarded as a dogmatist. This kind of reading certainly served polemical purposes. Another tradition that was hostile to Protagoras, and which was possibly partly connected to the sceptical interpretation, was the Epicurean tradition, which is responsible for the emphasis on the link between Protagoras and Democritus – in all likelihood, an unfounded idea. All in all, we must note that many – if not all – the testimonies we have about Protagoras are vitiated by underlying polemical attitudes of this sort, which in some cases lead to actual distortions of his thought. The history of this ancient reception must therefore be taken into account in order to come up with a suitable reconstruction.

Protagoras' pupils include Antimoerus of Mende, Carmidas and Euathlus of Athens, and Theodore of Cyrene. His influence has also been posited in relation to Prodicus, the so-called anonymous of Iamblichus and the *Dissoi logoi*, although it is difficult to measure its extent.

Gorgias of Leontini

Gorgias was born in Leontini (present-day Lentini), a Greek colony in Sicily, around 485 BC. He received his education in Sicily (he was reportedly a pupil of Empedocles, and some sources associate him with Thysias and Corax, traditionally regarded as the 'inventors' of rhetoric), although a life of travel led him to visit many cities and regions in Greece (Olympia, Delphi, Thessaly, Beotia, and Argos). Here he practised and taught rhetoric, achieving considerable success, including financially. Gorgias reached Athens in 427 BC, when he was despatched as an ambassador by his home city to discuss the delicate question of the war with Syracuse. It is said that, on this occasion, rhetoric too made its first entrance into Athens. He died a centenarian, probably in Larissa in Thessaly, at the end of a frugal life, 'never doing anything in view of pleasure' – as he once told an interlocutor.

Among Gorgias' most famous works we find the treatise *On Not-Being or on Nature*, which only survives thanks to two paraphrases, one by Sextus Empiricus and the other by the anonymous author of a text *On Melissus, Xenophanes, and Gorgias*. Some sources date this work to the 84th Olympics, which is to say between 444 and 441 BC, but this is dubious. No less complicated is the attempt to date other texts known to us: the two declamations *Encomium of Helen* and *Defence of*

Palamedes, which are among the few sophistic works to have survived; a long fragment from a *Funeral Oration* delivered in Athens, or at any rate written for an Athenian public; and the fragments of other orations delivered in various places in Greece. Gorgias may also have been the author of a treatise on *The Art of Rhetoric*, and of another text, *On the Opportune Moment* (*kairos*).

The names of many of Gorgias' pupils have been recorded: Alcidamas of Elea, Callicles of Acharnae, Isocrates of Athens, Licymnius of Chios, Meno of Larissa, Polus of Acragas, Protarcus of Athens, Proxenus of Thebes, and probably Lycophron too. Thucydides and Critias are also said to have been influenced by Gorgias, as was Aspasia, Pericles' *hetaira*.

Antiphon (of Rhamnous?)

Interest in Antiphon dates back to 1915, when a long papyrus fragment was brought to light (87B44 D.-K. = 37D38b L.-M.): whereas previously all that was known of the sophist were short and isolated quotes, the new discovery made available the longest surviving discussion of the opposition between *nomos* and *physis*, one of the most hotly debated topics in fifth-century Athens. This finding, however, raised the problem of Antiphon's identity: of whether the sophist by this name was to be identified with the rhetor who promoted the oligarchic coup of 411 BC. The first reconstruction of the fragment gave rise to the myth of Antiphon as a theorizer of equality and an ardent democrat, thereby ruling out the hypothesis that this author was the oligarch Antiphon. But then, in 1984, a new discovery proved the unfoundedness of the 'democratic' interpretations of the sophist. The demolition of the latter also removed the main obstacle to the unitary thesis, which currently seems to be the more reasonable one, even though it is impossible to prove it conclusively.[2] Clearly, if this is the correct hypothesis, what we have is a truly central figure on the political and intellectual scene in Athens, a personality whose importance is confirmed by the

[2] For an initial overview, I will refer to Bonazzi 2007: 52–6. Significantly, the two recent monographs by Hourcade 2001 and Gagarin 2002 favour the unitary reading; see also Decleva Caizzi 1969, Narcy 1989, and now Laks and Most 2016, vol. ix. Nevertheless, it is important to note with Woodruff 2004 that, however widespread this interpretation may be, it is not universally accepted: Pendrick 2002 once again supports the arguments of the separatists.

admiring description provided by Thucydides, who emphasizes the intelligence, eloquence, and boldness of the rhetor – the very qualities that represent defining features of the sophists, in both positive and negative terms.

From the surviving testimonies on the sophist and rhetor we know that he was born around 480 BC in the Attic deme of Rhamnous and that he received his early education from his father, Sophilus, whom the sources refer to as a 'sophist'. We know practically nothing of what happened to Antiphon after that, except for the fact that in Athens he acquired an ambiguous fame as a 'logographer' (that is, a writer of court speeches for private clients) and that for some time he worked in Corinth, where he promised to 'treat the suffering with speeches' (87A6 D.-K. = 37P10 L.-M.). Whereas Antiphon appears to have kept a low profile for most of his career, everything changed in the last, tumultuous years of his life: according to Thucydides' account, he was among the promoters of the secret coup which in 411 BC sought to introduce a more or less moderate form of oligarchy in Athens to replace the democratic regime. As is widely known, the coup failed, not least because of a lack of support from Sparta (which Antiphon reportedly visited as an ambassador). Many of the people involved fled, but not Antiphon, who delivered what Thucydides describes as 'the best defence ever offered up to my time in a trial for a capital crime' (8.68). Noteworthy as it was, the speech was not enough to save the sophist's life: Antiphon was sentenced to death, his property was seized, and his estates were razed.

Considering Antiphon's work as both a rhetor and a sophist, he is among the authors about whom we are most informed. From a philosophical perspective, the most relevant text is no doubt *On Truth*. This appears to revolve around the problem of *physis*, which is explored from various scientific and political points of view. In *On Concord*, a work addressed to a broader audience, Antiphon deals with ethical issues, giving proof of remarkable psychological acumen. Equal acumen is reflected in the fragments from the *Interpretation of Dreams*, which he based on rational methods. Too little survives of the *Statesman* to get an idea of the contents of this work, while all that is known of *On Agriculture* is the title. Particularly noteworthy among Antiphon's rhetorical works are the three *Tetralogies*, each of which consists of two accusatory speeches and two defensive speeches on fictional cases – probably exercises intended to explore legal (but also philosophical) problems. Tradition also credits him with a treatise entitled *The Art* (*of Rhetoric*) and with some *Prologues*. The most interesting works among the surviving orations are *On the Murder of Herodes*, *Against the Stepmother for Poisoning*, and *On the Choreutes*. We also have a fragment of what was probably the speech he gave to defend himself after the 411 BC coup. Finally, some sources identify the sophist Antiphon with another Antiphon, an author of tragedies: but this identification is made more problematic by the information that the poet was murdered by orders of the tyrant of Syracuse, Dionysius.

Xeniades of Corinth

A practically unknown figure, at different times Xeniades has been associated with Protagoras, Gorgias, Xenophanes, and the School of Elea, yet no reliable confirmation of any of these hypotheses has been found. His thesis that everything springs from nothing is certainly noteworthy and earned him an original place in the constellation of post-Parminedean thinkers.

Prodicus of Ceos

We know that Prodicus came from the island of Ceos in the Cyclades. The sources make no mention of his date of birth but nonetheless present him as a contemporary of Democritus, Socrates, Hippias, and Gorgias, which would suggest sometime around 460 BC. Like other sophists, Prodicus made repeated visits to Athens (where by 423 BC he was already well known) and other Greek cities, either as an emissary or to deliver speeches or lectures. One of the main reasons for his fame lies in his linguistic interests, and particularly in his ability to correctly distinguish the various meanings of terms, clarifying their nuances. Not without some irony, the importance of this research was acknowledged by Socrates (who at times went so far as to describe himself as a pupil of Prodicus) and Plato. These linguistic distinctions are based on the assumption that language can adequately reflect the variety of things: the correct use of names is therefore the precondition for an adequate evaluation of reality.

Prodicus also took an interest in natural problems (a record survives of a treatise *On Nature*), although he stands out for his humanistic emphasis, as is shown by his rationalist criticism of religion, according to which humans first deified all the natural forces on which their existence depended – such as the sun, the rivers, and the sea – and then the great benefactors who had contributed to the progress of civilization (for instance, Demeter and Dionysus for bread and wine). Finally, we know about the contents of a declamation entitled *The Choice of Heracles*,[3] in which the choice between vice and virtue provided an avenue to celebrate the freedom of human beings, who forge their own destiny. In the eyes of several interpreters, from Xenophon to George Grote, this call to sacrifice and virtue constitutes the most striking refutation of the charge of immorality directed against the sophists.

According to a late tradition, Prodicus died in Athens when he was charged with corrupting the young and forced to drink a cup of hemlock. Modern scholars have often dismissed this as an unreliable account; however, other sources report that he was expelled from a gymnasium for having addressed inappropriate words to the young: 'it is not impossible that he did have to face the kind of opposition which Protagoras spoke of as the common lot of all sophists'.[4]

Thrasymachus of Chalcedon

Thrasymachus was born in Chalcedon, a Bithynian city on the Bosphorus, around 460 BC. He chiefly devoted himself to rhetoric and composed several treatises, contributing to the development of the so-called mixed style and art prose. After arriving in Athens, possibly for the first time, in 427 BC, he became involved in local politics, albeit indirectly, given his status as a foreigner. In all likelihood, the long fragment from his speech *On the Constitution* was drafted in the context of the heated polemics that led to the coup of 411 BC. The reference to the constitution of the Athenian ancestors (starting from Solon), the so-called *Patrios politeia*, was one of the themes exploited by oligarchic propaganda (in particular that of its more moderate wing) in order to curb the growing power of Athenian demagogues (according to a different interpretation, however, this is a fragment of a speech that the sophist delivered in 407 BC in defence of his home city of Chalcedon, after a failed uprising against Athens). The fragment from the speech *For the People of Larissa* instead refers to the troubled

[3] Possibly part of the broader work entitled the *Seasons* (*Horai*): see p. 118, n. 35.

[4] Kerferd 1981a: 46.

political situation in Thessaly and puts forward a pan-Hellenic ideal for anti-Macedonian purposes.

However, Thrasymachus' fame is due not so much to the few surviving fragments of his writings as to Plato, who chose him as the protagonist of a memorable debate with Socrates in the first book of the *Republic*. The thesis defended by Thrasymachus, according to whom justice is nothing but the advantage of the stronger, constitutes a first expression of what later came to be described as 'political realism': there is a logic of force that imposes itself and imposes laws to serve one's self-interest, identifying the just with what contributes to asserting one's own power and interest. Justice, therefore, is no longer the principle capable of checking force, but rather a means to justify the predominance of those who find themselves in the stronger position. It remains to be ascertained, however, to what extent Thrasymachus actually endorsed theses of this sort. The source informing us of his suicide is dubious, and even the date of his death remains uncertain.

Hippias of Elis

Born in Elis, in the western Peloponnese, probably in 443 BC, Hippias was the first sophist to hail from a Doric city. He was widely admired (and generously remunerated) as a teacher and public speaker equipped with an astonishing memory, and served his city in many important diplomatic missions to Athens, Sparta, and Sicily. His political commitment also sealed his death, if we are to trust the report that he became involved with the democratic exiles fighting against the oligarchs in power in Elis (but it may be that our source here, Tertullian, is confusing the sophist with another famous Hippias, the son of the Athenian tyrant Peisistratos).

Hippias' career unfolded under the aegis of *polymathia*: his remarkable versatility enabled him not just to discuss the most disparate subjects – including astronomy and mathematics, music and poetry, painting and sculpture, history and mythology – in a large number of texts, but to distinguish himself in practical matters too. He wrote speeches (*epideixeis* such as the *Trojan Discourse*, along with actual orations), epic verses, tragedies, and dithyrambs. He also drew up lists of winners in the Olympics and various other catalogues – including ones of the names of various peoples, of the priestesses of Hera at Argos, and of philosophical doctrines. These interests are reflected in what is arguably Hippias' most important work, which is simply known as *Synagoge*, or *Collection*.

The sophist probably reached the height of his success at the time of his journey to Olympia, where he showed up wearing garments, footwear, and rings that he had crafted himself and which were no less beautiful than the most refined Persian jewels. Not only ancient authors (Plato) but also some modern interpreters have made some ironic remarks on Hippias' qualities, since it is difficult to take a man seriously who claims to be able to do everything on his own. Others, however, have praised the sophist of Elis for his all-round ideal of man, combining brightness of mind and manual dexterity. Be that as it may, Hippias' pursuits disprove the prejudice according to which the sophists were only interested in ethical and political matters. His many interests are not an empty show of erudition but proof of his desire to register the ongoing advances made by humankind in a wide range of areas. At least in this respect – namely his awareness of the historicity of the human experience – it is difficult to deny the importance of Hippias' contribution.

Critias of Athens

Critias' tomb was marked by a personification of oligarchy setting fire to democracy. In death as much as in life, Critias, the scion of one of Athens' noblest families and Plato's uncle, would appear to have ardently striven after a single goal: to bring down the popular regime he loathed. This loathing is a recurrent feature of his life, from his early youthful experiences (his involvement in the Hermes' mutilation in 415 BC and probably his joining of the coup of 411 BC) to the leading role he played in the much-despised government of the Thirty, which after the Spartan victory of 404 BC sought to turn Attica into a land of shepherds. He died fighting against the democrat Thrasybulus on Munichia in 403 BC.

A mark of infamy condemned Critias' work to an unjust oblivion; however, he gave proof of remarkable versatility, applying himself to a wide range of literary genres and carving out a prominent place for himself in the cultural life of Athens. Of particular note are his studies on the various *politeiai*, which combined an analysis of the type of constitution with an investigation into the most relevant aspects of civilian life and military organization. Many fragments survive of his political elegies and other poetic compositions, which were well suited to symposia. Critias also composed some tragedies, although in some cases their authorship is uncertain. He can probably be credited with the fragments from the *Tennes*, *Rhadamanthys*, and *Pirithous*, which appear to have explored the sharing – out of love and friendship – 'of the ultimate dangers, death or exile' – dangers whose full weight Critias bore in his own life.[5] The case of the satyr-play *Sisyphus* is more problematic, because it can also be attributed to Euripides.

Philostratus featured Critias in his *Lives of the Sophists*: for this reason, perhaps, Diels chose to include him in his edition; and since then he has always been reckoned among the sophists. However, if we rule out the fragments from the *Sisyphus*, there seem to be no cogent reasons to regard Critias as a sophist: he was not a teacher and appears to have championed a kind of old-fashioned, pro-Spartan education, essentially hostile to the teachings of the sophists (although some points of convergence between the two may be found). The importance that Critias assigned to poetry also seems to be at odds with the sophists' positions. Finally, even if one were to attribute the *Sisyphus* to him, this work is a theatrical text that cannot be taken to present doctrines personally endorsed by Critias. At most, like many other young Athenian nobles, he may be regarded as a pupil of the sophists (and of Socrates), but he can hardly be considered to have been a sophist himself.

Lycophron

Aristotle refers to Lycophron as a 'sophist': this is the only certain information we have about a figure of whom we otherwise know almost nothing – not where he came from, when he lived, or what his life was like. If the Lycophron mentioned by the anonymous author of the second Platonic letter (314d) were the sophist in question, we would know that he visited the court of Dionysius II in Sicily between 364 and 360 BC. Aristotle compares his style to that of Gorgias and Alcidamas, which has suggested the plausible conclusion that Lycophron was a pupil of Gorgias and a rough contemporary of Alcidamas. Lycophron would thus be a representative of the second

[5] Centanni 1997: 178.

generation of sophists. Our sources do not even record the titles of his works, although from the few testimonies we have it is possible to infer that he had a good command of the problems tackled by the most famous sophists – from the issue of language to the opposition between *nomos* and *physis*. This makes the lack of reliable information about him all the more regrettable.

Callicles of Acharnae

All we know about Callicles is what Plato tells us in the *Gorgias*. Some scholars have gone so far as to suggest that he is a fictional character. More reasonably, Dodds defended the opposite thesis, suggesting that Callicles truly existed but died young, thus leaving little memory of himself.[6] As far as we can judge from Plato's dialogue, he is reminiscent of another Athenian aristocrat, Critias. Like Critias, he is to be considered not so much a sophist as a pupil of the sophists – and Plato arguably used the figure of Callicles to illustrate the dangers of their theses.

Euthydemus and Dionysodorus of Chios

Most of the information that we have about these figures comes from Plato's *Euthydemus*; other testimonies from the *Cratylus* and Aristotle confirm that they were genuine historical figures. As far as we can tell, the distinctive feature of their work lies in their interest in sophisms, of which they make bold use in the Platonic dialogue. Ever since antiquity, this focus on paradoxical arguments has suggested a comparison with the Megarian School. Yet, there is no need, perhaps, to hypothesize, as Dorion 2009a does, that the two figures belonged to this school, thereby severing all links with the sophistic tradition. Rather – at any rate according to Plato's testimony – they represent the worst version of sophistry, the eristic type whose only goal was to win debates.

[6] Dodds 1959: 12–15. The hypothesis of a premature death is based on a prophecy *post eventum*, at *Gorgias*, 519a.

Alcidamas of Elaea

The only useful chronological information we have about Alcidamas is that, like Antisthenes and Lycophron, he was a pupil of Gorgias. He may indeed be regarded as a representative of the second generation of sophists, who appear to have focused almost exclusively on the art of rhetoric. He was probably one of the pupils of Gorgias most interested in the theme of improvisation, in contrast to those pupils (such as Isocrates) who instead privileged technical expertise and the drafting of written speeches. A trace of this contrast survives in the short speech entitled *On the Writers of Written Discourses or On the Sophists*. Along with a memorable sentence against slavery, Alcidamas is significantly associated with a speech entitled *Odysseus against the Treachery of Palamedes*: a work that, if genuine, would set him in competition with his master. Among the works now lost, the most important one is arguably *Museum*.

The *Dissoi logoi* and other anonymous treatises

Dissoi logoi (*Twofold Arguments* or *Pairs of Arguments*, as Laks and Most propose) is a text written in the Doric dialect that has been transmitted without a title or author as an appendix to the manuscripts of Sextus Empiricus, a sceptical philosopher lived under the Roman Empire. The title by which this text is known today comes from the opening words: 'Twofold arguments are spoken in Greece…'. A reference to the end of the Peloponnesian War appears to suggest a date between the late fifth and early fourth century BC, although this is a controversial hypothesis. No less controversial is the nature of the text: it has been taken to consist of school exercises, an orator's notes, an *epideixis*, or even notes taken by a listener. What is clearer is its structure, which consists 'in setting up opposing arguments about the identity or non-identity of apparently opposing moral and philosophical terms such as good and bad, true and false'.[7] Generally speaking, this text has not been very popular with modern scholars, who have often emphasized the banality of many of its arguments. However, its awareness of the relativity of any point of view and its tendency to arrange argu-

[7] Kerferd 1981a: 54.

ments into contrasting couples bear witness to 'the remarkable maturity of Greek thought in the second half of the fifth century'.[8] It is important to keep this point in mind when approaching the *Dissoi logoi*, which is one of the texts that best illustrates the Greeks' capacity to problematize reality.[9]

Along with the *Dissoi logoi*, there are a number of other anonymous texts that, according to scholars, can be traced back to the world of the sophists. Arguably the most interesting of these is the so-called *Anonymus Iamblichi*. Iamblichus (third–fourth century CE) was a Neoplatonist philosopher and the author of a work entitled *Protrepticus*, which includes long excerpts from previous authors (for instance, from Aristotle's *Protrepticus*). Scholars have identified roughly ten pages devoted to a defence of *nomos* that may be traced back to the fifth/fourth-century BC debate. What is also unique about this text is its focus on economic issues. Another text for which a sophistic origin has been suggested is part of an oration, *Against Aristogeiton*, preserved in Democritus' corpus: in this case too the topic discussed is the value of *nomos*. In both cases, however, it may be unwarranted to speak of a sophistic authorship; a more prudent approach would be to speak of texts influenced by sophistic themes. What may be inferred from these texts – without having to assign them to any specific sophist – is that the problems raised by the sophists continued to be debated for centuries.[10]

[8] Mazzarino 1966: 285–6.

[9] See also T. Robinson 1979 and Maso 2018.

[10] A succinct overview of the other anonymous treatises attributed to sophists may be found in Kerferd and Flashar 1998: 97–107.

APPENDIX 2: THE SOPHISTS AND SPECIALIST FORMS OF KNOWLEDGE (*TECHNAI*)

As we have repeatedly verified, competition with other 'intellectuals' was crucial for the sophists: while poets and philosophers were their primary targets, they engaged in an equally staunch polemic against the representatives of other forms of knowledge (the so-called *technai*), such as medicine, music, agriculture, and mathematics. The sophists affirmed the superiority of their teaching against such people as well. As far as we can tell, this claim was advanced in two different ways. In the case of Hippias (a famous polymath), and probably of Prodicus and Antiphon too, the sophists claimed to be as competent as specialists in a wide range of subjects: this explains the interest of sophists such as Hippias and Antiphon in geometrical problems (86B21 = 36D36L.-M.; 87B13 D.-K. = 37D 36a–b and R14–16 L.-M.), and Prodicus' focus on agriculture.[1]

In other cases, especially those of Protagoras and Gorgias, the competition with specialist forms of knowledge takes a far more heated form. While these sophists do not claim to have mastered specialist fields, they argue that their knowledge – the new knowledge of the sophists – allows them to prevail even over such fields. The *techne ton logon* – that is, the art of speeches taught by the sophists – allows them to take on the other *technai* in their own fields and even to gain the upper hand. Thus, in the *Gorgias*, Gorgias relates that, when he accompanied his brother, a physician, on his visits, he was often more successful than him – a specialist – in persuading patients to undergo treatment. From this he concludes that, in the presence of a public audience, rhetoric is capable of conquering specialist forms of knowledge: in the case of conflict, a layman will choose to be treated by a rhetor rather than a doctor (*Gorgias*, 456a–c). In Protagoras' case, too, we have sources attesting to a polemical engagement with the *technai*:

Not even this is true, that mensuration deals with perceptible and perishable magnitudes; for then it would have perished, when they perished. And astronomy also cannot be dealing with perceptible magnitudes nor with this heaven above us. For neither are perceptible lines such lines as the geometer speaks of (for no perceptible thing is straight or curved in this way; for a hoop touches a straight edge

[1] See Soverini 1998: 90–114; and Chapter 6, n. 34.

not at a point, but as Protagoras said it did, in his refutation of the geometers [that is along a line]).

(80B7 D.-K. partly reproduced by L.-M. as 31D33)[2]

Alongside geodesics, astronomy, and geometry, we cannot rule out medicine as a polemical target. One treatise from the *Hippocratic Corpus*, significantly entitled *The Art* (*peri technes*), polemically alludes to some unspecified 'professional slanderers', and it is tempting to see this as a reference to Protagoras (and possibly Gorgias as well[3]). Plato, too, reports this attitude in the *Sophist*, alluding to treatises by Protagoras on wrestling and other arts (232d–e = 80B8 D.-K. = 31D2 L.-M.). In all likelihood, the reference here is not to wrestling but to the capacity that Protagoras claimed to possess: the ability to 'contradict each individual expert in a given subject' – be it cosmology, theology, politics, or philosophy. As insightfully noted by Paolo Fait, these testimonies can also help clarify the meaning of what was probably Protagoras' most famous work, the *Kataballontes logoi* (*The Overthrower Arguments* or, better, *The Knockdown Arguments*), which contains the 'man-measure' thesis.[4] In this respect, it is worth quoting the following testimony on Pericles:

There is on record also a certain saying of Thucydides, the son of Melesias, touching the clever persuasiveness of Pericles, a saying uttered in jest. Thucydides belonged to the party of the 'Good and True', and was for a very long time a political antagonist of Pericles. When Archidamus, the king of the Lacedaemonians, asked him whether he or Pericles was the better wrestler, he replied: 'Whenever I throw him in wrestling (*katabalo palaion*), he, disputing the fall (*antilegon*), carries the point, and persuades the very men who saw him fall.'

(Plutarch, *Life of Pericles*, 8.3–4)

The presence of two key terms, the verbs *kataballo* and *antilego*, clearly suggests a Protagorean context. The *Kataballontes logoi*, therefore, are

[2] Let us also consider Philodemus' testimony: 'the <things> are not knowable, <the> words are not acceptable, <as> Protagoras indeed [*sc.* said] about ma<thematics>' (*PHerc.* 1676 = 80B7a D.-K. = 31D34 L.-M.). As regards the meaning of the polemic against geometry, we might posit (with Barnes 1979: ii.546) that in this case too Protagoras exploited his method of two contrasting *logoi*: geometry hinges on physical objects; now, if it does not deal with physical objects, all it amounts to is an insignificant verbal game; on the other hand, if it does deal with physical objects, it is subject to empirical evaluation; but any empirical evaluation is bound to offer different results from those provided by *a priori* analyses; thus even in relation to the apparent certainties of mathematics we find that for the same object there are two opposite *logoi*. Arguments of this sort were probably also used in the treatise *On Mathematics* (or *On the Sciences*) mentioned by Diogenes Laertius (80A1 D.-K. = 31D1 L.-M.). Besides, even in the *Protagoras* the sophist does not show himself to be very keen on the mathematical sciences (318d–e, 80A5 D.-K. = 31D37 L.-M.).

[3] See Jori 1996: 333–57.

[4] Fait 2007: xli.

those speeches or arguments that have the power to defeat one's opponent; and putting pupils in the condition to compete against anyone was the aim of antilogies.

An analysis of testimonies about the sophists' engagement with specialist forms of knowledge once again confirms their agonistic approach: through such polemics, they sought to present their teaching as superior to that of other specialists, be they poets, scientists, or philosophers.[5] This 'architectural' vocation – to quote an Aristotelian expression – of sophistic knowledge vis-à-vis all other forms of knowledge finds an exemplary expression in a statement attributed to Gorgias: 'Gorgias the orator said that those who neglect philosophy[6] but dedicate themselves to the ordinary disciplines (*ta enkuklia mathemata*) are similar to the suitors, who desired Penelope but slept with the maidservants' (82B29 D.-K. = 32P22 L.-M.) If we consider the ideological value that *technai* possessed in fifth-century democratic Athens, we once again realize just how provocative the sophists' activity was.

A reaction from the sophists' opponents, however, was not long in coming. The Hippocratic treatise *The Art* has already been mentioned; see for instance Chapter 1:

> Some there are who have made an art of vilifying the arts, though they consider, not that they are accomplishing the object I mention, but that they are making a display of their own knowledge. …To be eager to bring shame through the art of abuse upon the discoveries of others, improving nothing but disparaging before those who do not know the discoveries of those who do, seems to me to be not the ambition and work of intelligence, but the sign of a nasty nature, or of want of art.

To this one may add other texts from the *Corpus hippocraticum* (e.g. *On the Nature of Man*, 1–8) or certain passages from Plato (from the *Sophist* and *Euthydemus*) and Aristotle (especially from the *Sophistical Refutations*). Indeed, the specious nature of these polemics contributed to fuel the suspicion that the sophists were incompetent and merely eristic (from the Greek *eris*, 'discord') debaters: they were incompetent because they did not really grasp the things they were talking about, and merely eristic because they were only interested in winning debates. In certain cases, at least, it is difficult to dismiss these charges.

[5] In Protagoras' case, it seems as though a more open position was adopted in relation to music (or at any rate the musical theories of Damon, who was a representative of the 'new culture'): see Brancacci 2008.

[6] Evidently, the term 'philosophy' here refers to the kind of activity in which rhetors and sophists engaged.

BIBLIOGRAPHY

Journal titles are abbreviated as in *L'Année philologique*.

1. Editions and translations

Barnes, Jonathan (ed.) 1984. *The Complete Works of Aristotle*. 2 vols. Princeton, NJ, Princeton University Press.

Bonazzi, Mauro 2007. *I sofisti*. Milan, Rizzoli.

Cooper, John (ed.) 1997. *Plato. Complete Works*. Indianapolis, IN, and Cambridge, Hackett Publishing Company.

Diels, Hermann, and Kranz, Walter 1951–2. *Die Fragmente der Vorsokratiker*. Sixth edition, Berlin, Weidmann.

Dillon, John, and Gergel, Tania 2003. *The Greek Sophists*. London, Penguin.

Freeman, Kathryn 1948. *Ancilla to the Pre-Socratic Philosophers. A Complete Translation of the Fragments in Diels' 'Fragmente der Vorsokratiker'*. Oxford, Blackwell.

Kent Sprague, Rosamund (ed.) 1972. *The Older Sophists*. Columbia, SC, University of South Carolina Press.

Laks, André, and Most, Glenn W. 2016. *Early Greek Philosophy*. 9 vols. Cambridge, MA, Harvard University Press.

———, and ——— 2016. *Les débuts de la philosophie. Des premiers penseurs grecs à Socrate*. Paris, Fayard.

Pradeau, Jean-François (ed.) 2009. *Les sophistes*. With the assistance of M. Bonazzi, L. Brisson, M.-L. Desclos, L.-A. Dorion, A. Macé, and M. Patillon. 2 vols. Paris, Flammarion.

Untersteiner, Mario 1949–62. *I sofisti. Testimonianze e frammenti*. With the assistance of A. M. Battegazzore. 4 vols. Florence, La Nuova Italia.

2. Works cited

Alvoni, Giovanna 2017. 'Die Rhesis des Sisyphos über den Ursprung der Religion (Kritias, Fr. 19 Sn.-K.)', *Paideia* 72: 467–81.

Apfel, Lauren J. 2011. *The Advent of Pluralism. Diversity and Conflict in the Age of the Sophists*. Oxford, Oxford University Press.

Arrighetti, Graziano 1998. *Esiodo. Opere*. Turin, Utet.

Balaudé, Jean-François 2006. 'Hippias le passeur', in Sassi 2006: 287–304.

Balla, Chloe 2018. 'πέφυκε πλεονεκτεῖν? Plato and the Sophists on Greed and Savage Humanity', *Polis* 35: 83–101.

Barnes, Jonathan 1979. *The Presocratic Philosophers*. 2 vols. London, Routledge.

Barney, Rachel 2017. 'Callicles and Thrasymachus', in E. N. Zalta (ed.), *The Stanford Encyclopedia of Philosophy* (Fall 2017 edition), <https://plato.stanford.edu/archives/fall2017/entries/callicles-thrasymachus/>

Bastianini, Guido, and Decleva Caizzi, Fernanda 1989. *'Antipho', in Corpus dei papiri filosofici greco e romani*, vol. I.1. Florence, Olschki: 176–222.

Beresford, Adam 2013. 'Fangs, Feathers, & Fairness: Protagoras on the Origins of Right and Wrong', in Ophuijsen, Van Ralte, and Stork 2013: 139–62.

Betegh, Gábor 2006. 'Greek Philosophy and Religion', in M. L. Gill and P. Pellegrin (eds.), *A Companion to Ancient Philosophy*. Oxford, Blackwell: 625–39.

Bett, Richard 1989. 'The Sophists and Relativism'. *Phronesis* 34: 139–69.

——— 2002. 'Is There a Sophistic Ethics?' *AncPhil* 22: 235–61.

Blank, David 1985. 'Socratics Versus Sophists on Payment for Teaching', *ClAnt* 4: 1–49.

Bonazzi, Mauro 2004. 'Atene, i sofisti e la democrazia: Protagora e i suoi critici', *PPol* 27: 333–59.

——— 2006a. 'La realtà, la legge, la concordia secondo Antifonte', *QS* 64: 117–39.

——— 2006b. 'L'uomo, gli dei, le bestie: a proposito dell'antropologia di Antifonte', *Elenchos* 27: 101–15.

——— 2008. 'Thrasymaque, la polis et le dieux', *PhilosAnt* 8: 61–84.

——— 2009a. 'Antifonte, Socrate e i maestri d'infelicità', *EPlaton* 6: 25–39.

——— 2009b. 'Protagoras', in Pradeau 2009a: i.43–90, 443–72.

——— 2011. 'Il mito di Prometeo nel *Protagora*: una variazione sul tema delle origini', in F. Calabi and S. Gastaldi (eds.). Sankt Augustin, Academia Verlag, pp. 41–57.

——— 2012. 'Antifonte presocratico', *Elenchos* 23: 21–40.

——— 2016. 'Antiphon le "philochrematos"', in E. Helmer (ed.), *Richesse et pauvreté chez les philosophes de l'antiquité*. Paris, Vrin: 47–58.

——— 2017. *Atene, la città inquieta*. Turin, Einaudi.

——— 2018. *Processo a Socrate*. Rome, Laterza.

——— 2020. 'Ethical and Political Thought in Antiphon's *Truth* and *Concord*', in D. Wolfsdorf (ed.), *Early Greek Thought*. Oxford, Oxford University Press, forthcoming.

——— and Pradeau, Jean-François 2009. 'Lycophron', in Pradeau 2009a: i.333–41, 522–5.

Brancacci, Aldo 1996. 'Protagora e la critica letteraria', in M. S. Funghi (ed.), *Odoi dizesios. Le vie della ricerca. Studi in onore di Francesco Adorno*. Florence, Olschki: 109–19.

——— 2002a. 'Protagora e la *techne sophistike*: Plat. *Prot.* 316d–317c', *Elenchos* 23: 11–32.

——— 2002b. 'Protagoras, l'*orthoepeia* et la justesse de noms', in A. Brancacci and M. Dixsaut (eds.), *Platon source de présocratiques*. Paris, Vrin: 169–90.

——— 2004. 'Il *logos* di Ippia: Plat. *Prot.* 337c–338b', in G. Casertano (ed.), *Il Protagora di Platone. Struttura e problematiche.* Naples, Loffredo: 390–401.

——— 2008. 'Protagora, Damone e la musica', in *Musica e filosofia da Damone a Filodemo*. Florence, Olschki: 21–33.

Brisson, Luc 1994. 'Diagoras de Mélos', in Goulet 1989–2018: ii.750–7.

——— 2009. 'Critias', in Pradeau 2009a: i.391–442, 545–58.

Brunschwig, Jacques 1984. 'Hippias d'Élis, philosophe-ambassadeur', in Greek Philosophical Society 1984: 269–76.

——— 2002. 'Democritus and Xeniades', in Caston and Graham 2002: 159–67.

Buchheim, Thomas 1989. *Gorgias von Leontinoi. Reden, Fragmente, und Testimonien.* Hamburg, Meiner.

Bultrighini, Umberto 1999. '*Maledetta democrazia*'. *Studi su Crizia.* Alessandria, Edizioni dell'Orso.

Burkert, Walter 1985a. *Greek Religion.* London, Blackwell (first published Stuttgart 1977).

——— 1985b. 'Herodot über die Namen der Götter: Polytheismus als historisches Problem', *MH* 42: 121–32.

Burnyeat, Myles 1976. 'Protagoras and Self-Refutation in Later Greek Philosophy', *PhR* 85: 44–69.

Calogero, Guido 1932. *Studi sull'Eleatismo.* Florence, La Nuova Italia.

Canfora, Luciano 2001. *Storia della letteratura greca.* Rome and Bari, Laterza.

Capra, Andrea 1997. 'La tecnica di misurazione del *Protagora*', *ASNP*, 4th series, 2: 273–327.

——— 2005. 'Protagoras' Achilles: Homeric Allusions as a Satirical Weapon (Plat. *Prot.* 340A)', *CPh* 100: 274–7.

Casertano, Gianni 1971. *Natura e istituzioni umane nelle dottrine dei sofisti.* Florence and Naples, Il tripode.

——— 1986. 'L'amour entre "logos" et "pathos": quelques considérations sur "l'Hélène" de Gorgias', in Cassin 1986: 211–20.

——— 2004. *Sofista.* Naples, Guida.

Cassin, Barbara 1980. *Si Parmenide. Le traité anonyme De Melisso Xenophane et Gorgia.* Lille, Presses universitaires de Lille.

——— (ed.) 1986. *Positions de la sophistique.* Paris, Vrin.

——— 1995. *L'effet sophistique.* Paris, Gallimard.

Castagnoli, Luca 2010. *Ancient Self-Refutation. The Logic and History of the Self-Refutation Argument from Democritus to Augustine.* Cambridge, Cambridge University Press.

Caston, Victor 2002. 'Gorgias on Thought and Its Objects', in Caston and Graham 2002: 205–32.

——— and Graham Daniel W. (eds.) 2002. *Presocratic Philosophy. Essays in Honour of A.P.D. Mourelatos.* Aldershot, Ashgate.

Centanni, Monica 1997. '*Atene assoluta. Crizia dalla tragedia alla storia*', Padua, Esedra.

Classen, Carl J. 1976. 'The Study of Language Amongst Socrates' Contemporaries', in C. J. Classen (ed.), *Sophistik*. Darmstadt, Wissenschaftliche Buchgesellschaft: 215–47.

Classen, Carl J. 1981. 'Aristotle's Picture of the Sophists', in Kerferd 1981b: 7–24.

Cole, Thomas 1991. *The Origins of Rhetoric in Ancient Greece*. Baltimore, MD, and London, The Johns Hopkins University Press.

Collette Bernard, Gavray Marc-Antoine, and Narbonne J.-M. (eds.) 2019. *L'esprit critique de l'antiquité I. Critique et licence dans la Grèce antique*. Paris, Les Belles Lettres.

Consigny, Scott 1994. 'Nietzsche's Reading of the Sophists', *RhetR* 13: 5–26.

——— 2001. *Gorgias, Sophist and Artist*, Columbia, SC, University of South Carolina Press.

Corey, David 2015. *The Sophists in Plato's Dialogues*. Albany, NY: State University of New York Press.

Corradi, Michele 2006. 'Protagora e *l'orthoepeia* nel *Cratilo* di Platone', in G. Arrighetti and M. Tulli (eds.), *Esegesi letteraria e riflessione sulla lingua nella cultura greca*. Pisa, Giardini Stampatori: 47–63.

——— 2007a. 'Protagoras dans son contexte. L'homme mesure et la tradition archaïque de l'*incipit*', *Mètis* 5: 185–204.

——— 2007b. 'Protagora e la forza del discorso: la tradizione sull'*epangelma*'. *SemRom* 10: 277–91.

——— 2012. *Protagora tra filologia e filosofia. La testimonianza di Aristotele*. Pisa, Fabrizio Serra Editore.

——— 2017. 'Il περὶ θεῶν di Protagora. Un nuovo tentativo di ricostruzione', *Maia* 69: 444–69.

Crane, Gregory 1998. *Thucydides and the Ancient Simplicity. The Limits of Political Realism*. Berkeley, CA, University of California Press.

Curd, Patricia 2006. 'Gorgias and the Eleatics', in Sassi 2006: 183–200.

Decleva Caizzi, Fernanda 1969. *Antiphontis Tetralogiae*. Milan, Cisalpino.

——— 1978. 'Il frammento 1 D.-K. di Protagora: nota critica', *Acme* 31: 11–35.

——— 1985. 'Ricerche su Antifonte: a proposito di *POxy* 1364 fr. 1', in M. Capasso, F. De Martino, and P. Rosati (eds.), *Studi di filosofia preplatonica*. Naples, Bibliopolis: 191–208.

——— 1986a. '"Hysteron proteron": la nature et la loi selon Antiphon et Platon', *RMM* 91: 291–310.

——— 1986b. 'Il nuovo papiro di Antifonte', in F. Adorno, F. Decleva Caizzi, F. Lasserre, and F. Vendruscolo (eds.), *Protagora, Antifonte, Posidonio Aristotele. Saggi su frammenti inediti e nuove testimonianze da papyri*. Florence, Olschki: 61–9.

——— 1999: 'Protagoras and Antiphon: Sophistic Debates on Justice', in A. A. Long (ed.), *The Cambridge Companion to Early Greek Philosophy*. Cambridge, Cambridge University Press: 311–31.

Demont, Paul 1993. 'La formule de Protagoras "L'homme est la mesure de toutes choses"', in *Problèmes de la morale antique*. Amiens, Faculté des lettres: 39–58.

Denyer, Nicholas 2013. 'The Political Skill of Protagoras', in Harte and Lane 2013: 155–67.

De Romilly, Jacqueline 1973. 'Gorgias et le pouvoir de la poésie', *JHS* 93: 155–72.

——— 1975. *Magic and Rhetoric in Ancient Greece*. Cambridge, MA, Harvard University Press.

——— 1986. 'Les manies de Prodicus et la rigeur de la langue grecque', *MH* 43: 1–18.

——— 1988. *Les grands sophistes dans l'Athènes de Périclès*. Paris, Éditions du Fallois.

——— 2005. *La legge nel pensiero greco. Dalle origini ad Aristotele*. Milan, Garzanti (first published as *La loi dans la pensée grecque. Des origines à Aristote*. Paris, Les Belles Lettres, 1971).

Detienne, Marcel 2006. *Les maîtres de vérité dans la Grèce archaïque*. Second edition, Paris, Librairie Générale Française (first published 1967).

Di Benedetto, Vincenzo 1955. 'Il Περὶ τοῦ μὴ ὄντος di Gorgia e la polemica contro Protagora', *RAL* 10: 287–307.

——— 2001. 'Contributo al testo del frammento di Protagora sugli dei', *RCCM* 43: 345–6.

Diels, Hermann 1884. '*Gorgias und Empedokles*', *Sitzungsberichte der Königlich Preußischen Akademie der Wissenschaften zu Berlin*: 343–68 (reprinted in C. J. Classen (ed.), *Sophistik*. Darmstadt, Wissenschaftliche Buchgesellschaft, 1976: 351–83).

Dihle, Albrecht 1977. 'Das Satyrspiel Sisyphos', *Hermes* 105: 28–42.

Dodds, Eric R. 1951. *The Greeks and the Irrational*. Berkeley, CA, University of California Press.

——— 1959. *Plato. Gorgias. A Revised Text with Introduction and Commentary*. Oxford, Oxford University Press.

——— 1973. 'The Sophistic Movement and the Failure of Greek Liberalism', in *The Ancient Concept of Progress and Other Essays on Greek Literature and Belief*. Oxford, Clarendon Press: 92–105.

Dorion, Louis-André 2008. 'Héraclès entre Prodicos et Xenophon', *PhilosAnt* 8: 85–114.

——— 2009a. 'Euthydème et Dionysodore', in Pradeau 2009a: ii.63–80, 179–87.

——— 2009b. 'Prodicos', in Pradeau 2009a: i.343–72, 525–39.

Drozdek, Adam 2005. 'Protagoras and the Instrumentality of Religion', *AC* 74: 41–50.

Dumont, Jean-Paul 1986. 'Prodicos: de la méthode au système', in Cassin 1986: 221–32.

Edmunds, Lowell 2006. 'What Was Socrates Called?', *CQ* 56: 414–25.

Ehrenberg, Victor 1957. *Sophocles and Pericles*. London, Blackwell.

El Murr, Dimitri 2019. 'Platon contre (et avec) Thrasymaque', in Collette, Gavray, and Narbonne 2019: 343–64.

Fait, Paolo 2007. *Aristotele. Le confutazioni sofistiche*. Rome and Bari, Laterza.

Farrar, Cynthia 1988. *The Origins of Democratic Thinking*. Cambridge, Cambridge University Press.

Fowler, Ryan C. 2014. *Plato in the Third Sophistic*. Berlin, Walter de Gruyter.

Furley, David 1981. 'Antiphon's Case Against Justice', in Kerferd 1981b: 81–91.

Fussi, Alessandra 2006. *Retorica e potere. Una lettura del Gorgia di Platone*. Pisa, ETS.

Gagarin, Michael 1994. 'Probability and Persuasion: Plato and Early Greek Rhetoric', in I. Worthington (ed.), *Persuasion. Greek Rhetoric in Action*. London, Routledge: 46–68.

——— 2001. 'Did the Sophists Aim to Persuade?', *Rhetorica* 19: 275–91.

——— 2002. *Antiphon the Athenian. Oratory, Law, and Justice in the Age of the Sophists*. Austin, TX, University of Texas Press.

——— 2007. 'Rational Argument in Early Athenian Oratory', in J. Powell (ed.), *Logos. Rational Argument in Classical Rhetoric*. London, Institute of Classical Studies: 9–18.

——— 2008. 'Protagoras et l'art de la parole', *PhilosAnt* 8: 23–32.

Gavray, Marc-Antoine 2016. 'De l'Anonyme à Jamblique: ou de l'usage politique de la richesse', in É. Helmer (ed.), *Richesse et pauvreté chez les philosophes de l'antiquité*. Paris, Vrin: 277–303.

——— 2017. *Platon, héritier de Protagoras. Un dialogue sur les fondements de la démocratie*. Paris, Vrin.

Gigon, Olof 1985. 'Il libro "Sugli dei" di Protagora', *RSF* 40: 419–48.

Giuliano, Fabio M. 1998. 'Un dimenticato frammento di poetica: *POxy* III 414 e l'"enciclopedia del sapere"', in *Papiri filosofici. Miscellanea di studi II*. Florence, Olschki: 115–65.

Goldhill, Simon 1986. *Reading Greek Tragedy*. Cambridge, Cambridge University Press.

Gomperz, Heinrich 1912. *Sophistik und Rhetorik*. Berlin and Leipzig, Wissenschaftliche Buchgesellschaft.

Goulet, Richard (ed.) 1989–2018. *Dictionnaire des philosophes antiques*. 7 vols. Paris, Éditions du CNRS.

Gray, Vivienne 2006. 'The Linguistic Philosophies of Prodicus in Xenophon's "Choice of Heracles"?', *CQ*, 56: 426–35.

——— 2007. Xenophon on Government. Cambridge, Cambridge University Press.

Greek Philosophical Society 1984. *The Sophistic Movement*. Athens, Athenian Library of Philosophy.

Grote, George 1864. *A History of Greece. From the Earliest Period to the Close of the Generation Contemporary with Alexander the Great*. London, Routledge.

Gourinat, Jean-Baptiste 2019. 'L'athéisme antique, entre accusation et réalité', in Collette, Gavray, and Narbonne 2019: 167–89.

Guthrie, William K. C. 1971. *The Sophists*. Cambridge, Cambridge University Press (first published 1969 as part 1 of *A History of Greek Philosophy*, vol. 3, Cambridge, Cambridge University Press).

Harte, Verit, and Lane, Melissa (eds.) 2013. *Politeia in Greek and Roman Philosophy*. Cambridge, Cambridge University Press.

Heinimann, Felix 1945. *Nomos und Physis. Herkunft und Bedeutung einer Antithese im griechischen Denken des 5. Jahrhunderts*. Basel, Schweizerischen Beiträge zur Altertumswissenschaft.

Henrichs, Albert 1975. 'Two Doxographical Notes: Democritus and Prodicus on Religion', *HSCPh* 79: 93–123.

——— 1976. 'The Atheism of Prodicus', *CErc* 6: 15–21.

Hobbs, Angela 2000. *Plato and the Hero. Courage, Manliness and the Impersonal Good*. Cambridge, Cambridge University Press.

Hoffmann, Klaus F. 1997. *Das Recht im Denken der Sophistik*. Stuttgart and Leipzig, Teubner.

Horky, Phillip S. 2006. 'The Imprint of the Soul: Psychosomatic Affection in Plato, Gorgias, and the "Orphic" Gold Tablets', *Mouseion* 6: 383–98.

Hourcade, Annie 2001. *Antiphon d'Athènes. Une pensée de l'individu*. Brussels, Ousia.

——— 2006. *Sophistique et atomisme*. Brussels, Ousia.

Iannucci, Alessandro 2002. *La parola e l'azione. I frammenti simposiali di Crizia*. Bologna, Edizioni Nautilus.

Ioli, Roberta (ed. and trans.) 2010. *Gorgia. Su ciò che non è*. Zürich and New York, Olms.

——— 2013. *Gorgia. Testimonianze e frammenti*. Rome, Carocci.

Isnardi Parente, Margherita 1969. 'Il pensiero politico greco dalle origini alla sofistica: Socrate e Platone', in L. Firpo (ed.), *Storia delle idee politiche, economiche e sociali. Vol. I*. Turin, Utet: 127–289.

——— 1977. *Sofistica e democrazia antica*. Florence, Sansoni.

Jaeger, Werner 1947. *The Theology of the Early Greek Philosophers*. Oxford, Clarendon Press.

Jori, Alberto 1996. *Medicina e medici nell'antica Grecia. Saggio sul peri technes ippocratico*. Bologna, Il Mulino.

Kahn, Charles 1973. *The Verb 'Be' in Ancient Greek*. Dordrecht, Reidel.

——— 1981. 'The Origins of Social Contract Theory', in Kerferd 1981b: 92–108.

——— 1997. 'Greek Religion and Philosophy in the Sisyphus Fragment', *Phronesis* 42: 247–62.

Kennedy, George A. 1963. *The Art of Persuasion in Greece*. Princeton, NJ, Princeton University Press.

Kerferd, George B. 1955–6. 'Gorgias on Nature or What is Not', *Phronesis* 1: 3–25.

——— 1981a. *The Sophistic Movement*, Cambridge, Cambridge University Press.

——— (ed.) 1981b. *The Sophists and Their Legacy*. Wiesbaden, Steiner Verlag.

——— 1984. 'Meaning and Reference: Gorgias and the Relation Between Language and Reality', in Greek Philosophical Society 1984: 215–22.

——— 1985. 'Gorgias and Empedocles', *Syculorum Gymnasium* 38: 595–605.

——— and Flashar, Helmut 1998. 'Die Sophistik', in F. Überweg and H. Flashar (eds.), *Grundriss der Geschichte der Philosophie. Die Philosophie der Antike, vol. 2.1: Sophistik, Sokrates, Sokratik, Mathematik, Medizin.* Basel, Schwabe: 1–137.

Kuntz, Mary 1993. 'The Prodikean "Choice of Herakles": AReshaping of Myth', *CJ* 89: 163–81.

Lapini, Walter 1997. *Commento all'Athenaion Politeia dello pseudo-Senofonte.* Florence, Dipartimento di Scienze dell'Antichità 'Giorgio Pasquali'.

Lee, Mi-Kyoung 2005. *Epistemology After Protagoras. Responses to Relativism in Plato, Aristotle, and Democritus.* Oxford, Clarendon Press.

Lloyd, Geoffrey E. R. 1979. *Magic, Reason and Experience. Studies in the Origins and Development of Greek Science.* Cambridge, Cambridge University Press.

——— 1987. *The Revolutions of Wisdom. Studies in the Claims and Practices of Ancient Greek Science.* Berkeley, CA, University of California Press.

Long, Anthony A. 1984. 'Methods of Argument in Gorgias' Palamedes', in Greek Philosophical Society 1984: 233–41.

——— 2015. *Greek Models of Mind.* Cambridge, MA: Harvard University Press.

Macé, Arnaud 2008. 'Un monde sans pitiè: Platon à l'échole de Thasymaque de Chalcédoine', *PhilosAnt* 8: 33–60.

——— 2009. 'Thrasymaque', in Pradeau 2009a: ii.7–28, 149–66.

Mansfeld, Jaap 1981. 'Protagoras on Epistemological Obstacles and Persons', in Kerferd 1981b: 38–53.

——— 1985. 'Historical and Philosophical Aspects of Gorgias' "On What Is Not"', *SicGymn* 38: 243–71.

——— 1986. 'Aristotle, Plato, and the Preplatonic Doxography and Chronography', in G. Cambiano (ed.), *Storiografia e dossografia nella filosofia antica.* Turin, Tirrenia Stampatori: 1–59.

——— 1988. '*De Melisso Xenophane Gorgia*: Pyrrhonizing Aristotelianism', *RM* 131: 239–76.

Manuwald, Bernd 2013. 'Protagoras' Myth in Plato's *Protagoras*: Fiction or Testimony?', in Ophuijsen, Van Ralte, and Stork 2013: 163–77.

Maso, Stefano 2018. *Dissoi logoi.* Rome, Edizioni di storia e letteratura.

Mayhew, Robert (ed. and trans.) 2011. *Prodicus the Sophist.* Texts, translations, and commentary. Oxford, Oxford University Press.

Mazzara, Giuseppe 1999. *Gorgia. La retorica del verosimile.* Sankt Augustin, Akademia Verlag.

——— 2005. 'La rhétorique éléatico-gorgienne d'Alcidamas chez Diogène Laërce (IX, 54) et le quatre fonctions fondamentales du λόγος', *AC* 74: 51–67.

Mazzarino, Santo 1966. *Il pensiero storico classico*, vol. 1. Bari, Laterza.

Momigliano, Arnaldo 1930. 'Prodico di Ceo e le dottrine sul linguaggio da Democrito ai Cinici', *Atti della Regia Accademia delle Scienze di Torino* 65: 95–107.

Morgan, Kathryn 2000. *Myth and Philosophy from the Presocratics to Plato.* Cambridge, Cambridge University Press.

Most, Glenn W. 1986. 'Sophistique et herméneutique', in Cassin 1986: 233–45.

Mourelatos, Alexander P. D. 1985. 'Gorgias on the Functions of Language', *SicGymn* 38: 607–30.

Muir, J. V. 1985. 'Religion and the New Education: The Challenge of the Sophists', in P. E. Easterling and J. V. Muir (eds.), *Greek Religion and Society*. Cambridge, Cambridge University Press: 191–218.

Musti, Domenico 1995. *Demokratía. Origini di un'idea*. Rome, Laterza.

Nails, Debra 2002. *The People of Plato*. Indianapolis, IN, and Cambridge, Hackett.

Narcy, Michel 1989. 'Antiphon d'Athènes', in Goulet 1989–2018: i.225–44.

——— 1996. 'Les interprétations de la pensée politique d'Antiphon au XXe siècle', *RFHIP* 3: 31–45.

Natali, Carlo 1986. 'Aristote et les méthodes d'enseignement de Gorgias', in Cassin 1986: 105–16.

Neschke-Hentschke, Ada 1995. *Platonisme politique et théproe du droit naturel. Contributions à une archéologie de la culture politique européenne. Vol. I. Le platonisme politique dans l'antiquité*. Louvain and Paris, Éditions Peeters.

Nestle, Wilhelm 1922. 'Die Schrift des Gorgias 'Über die Natur oder Über das Nichtseiende'', *Hermes* 57: 551–62.

——— 1936. 'Die *Horen* des Prodikos', *Hermes* 71: 151–70.

——— 1948. '*Critias*', in *Griechischen Studien*. Stuttgart, Hansmann: 253–320.

Newiger, Hans-Joachim 1973. *Untersuchungen zu Gorgias Schrift über das Nichtseiende*. Berlin, De Gruyter.

Nietzsche, Friedrich 1964. *The Will to Power*, trans. W. A. Kaufmann. New York: Vintage (first published in German 1901).

Ophuijsen Johan M. van, Van Ralte Marleen, and Stork Peter (eds.) 2013. *Protagoras of Abdera. The Man, His Measure*. Leiden, Brill.

Ostwald, Martin 1969. *Nomos and the Beginnings of the Athenian Democracy*. Oxford, Oxford University Press.

——— 1986. *From Popular Sovereignty to the Sovereignty of Law. Law, Society, and Politics in Fifth-Century Athens*. Berkeley, CA, University of California Press.

——— 1990. '*Nomos* and *Physis* in Antiphon's *Peri aletheias*', in M. Griffith and D. J. Mastronarde (eds.), *Cabinets of the Muses*. Atlanta, GA, Scholars Press: 293–306.

O'Sullivan, Neil 1996. 'Written and Spoken in the First Sophistic', in I. Worthington (ed.), *Voice into Text. Orality and Literacy in Ancient Greece*, Leiden, Brill: 115–27.

Paci, Enzo 1957. *Storia del pensiero presocratico*. Rome, ERI.

Palmer, John 1999. *Platos' Reception of Parmenides*. Oxford, Oxford University Press.

——— 2009. *Parmenides and Presocratic Philosophy*. Oxford, Oxford University Press.

Palumbo, Lidia 2005. 'Sul riferimento alla teologia di Senofane nel *Sisifo satiresco*', in M. Bugno (ed.), *Senofane ed Elea tra Ionia e Magna Grecia*. Naples, Luciano editore: 77–86.

Patzer, Andreas 1986. *Der Sophist Hippias als Philosophiehistoriker*. Freiburg im Breisgau and Munich, Alber.

Patzer, Harald 1974. 'Der Tyrann Kritias und die Sophistik', in K. Döring and W. Kullmann, *Studia Platonica: Festschrift für Hermann Gundert*. Amsterdam, B.R. Grüner: 41–8.

Pendrick, Gerard 2002. *Antiphon the Sophist. The Fragments*. Cambridge, Cambridge University Press.

Pfeiffer, Rudolf 1968. *History of Classical Scholarship. From the Beginnings to the End of the Hellenistic Age*. Oxford, Clarendon Press.

Pernot, Laurent 2006. *La retorica dei Greci e dei Romani*. Palermo, Palumbo.

Popper, Karl R. 1971. *The Open Society and Its Enemies*. Princeton, NJ, Princeton University Press.

Poulakos, John 1983. 'Gorgias' *Encomium to Helen* and the Defense of Rhetoric', *Rhetorica* 1: 1–16.

Pradeau, Jean-François (ed.) 2009a. *Les sophistes*. With the assistance of M. Bonazzi, L. Brisson, M.-L. Desclos, L.-A. Dorion, A. Macé, and M. Patillon. 2 vols. Paris, Flammarion.

Pradeau, Jean-François (ed.) 2009b. 'Xéniade', in Pradeau 2009a: i.327–31, 520–1.

Rademaker, Adriaan 2013. 'The Most Correct Account: Protagoras on Language', in Ophuijsen, van Raalte and Stork 2013: 87–111.

Robinson, John M. 1973. 'On Gorgias', in E. N. Lee, A. P. D. Mourelatos, and R. M. Rorty (eds.), *Exegesis and Argument*. Assen, Van Gorcum: 49–60.

Robinson, Thomas M. 1979. *Contrasting Arguments. An edition of the Dissoi logoi*, New York, Arno Press.

Rocca-Serra, Guillaume, 1990. 'Naissance de l'exégèse allégorique et naissance de la raison', in J.-F. Mattei (ed.), *La naissance de la raison en Grèce*. Paris, Presses universitaires de France: 77–82.

Romeyer-Dherbey, Gilbert 1985. *Les Sophistes*. Paris, Presses universitaires de France.

Rorty, Richard 1979. *Philosophy and the Mirror of Nature*. Princeton, NJ, Princeton University Press.

Rosenmeyer, Thomas G. 1955. 'Gorgias, Aeschylus and *Apate*', *AJPh* 1955: 225–60.

Sansone, David 2004. 'Heracles at the Y', *JHS* 124: 125–42.

Santoro, Mariacarolina 1997. 'Il fr. 19 Snell del *Sisifo* di Crizia come testimonianza della concezione socratica del divino: Crizia "accusatore" di Socrate?', *Elenchos* 18: 257–76.

Sassi Maria Michela (ed.) 2006. *La costruzione del discorso filosofico nell'età dei presocratici*. Pisa, Edizioni della Normale.

——— (ed.) 2013. 'Where Epistemology and Religion Meet: What Do(es) God(s) Look Like?', *Rhizai* 12: 283–307.

Saunders, Trevor J. 1981. 'Protagoras and Plato on Punishment', in Kerferd 1981b: 129–41.

Schiappa, Edward 1991. *Protagoras and Logos*. Columbia, SC, University of South Carolina Press.

Scholten, Helga 2003. *Die Sophistik. Eine Bedrohnung für die Religion und Politik der Polis?* Berlin, Akademie Verlag.

Scodel, Ruth 1980. *The Trojan Trilogy of Euripides*. Göttingen, Vandenhoek & Ruprecht.

Sedley, David 2013. 'The Atheist Underground', in Harte and Lane 2013: 329–48.

Segal, Charles 1962. 'Gorgias and the Psychology of Logos', *HSCPh* 66: 99–155.

Sihvola, Juha 1989. *Decay, Progress, the Good Life? Hesiod and Protagoras on the Development of Culture*. Helsinki, Societas Scientiarum Fennica.

Solmsen, Friedrich 1931. *Antiphonstudien. Untersuchungen zur Enstehung der attischen Gerichtsrede*. Berlin, Weidmann.

——— 1975. *Intellectual Experiments of the Greek Enlightenment*. Princeton, NJ, Princeton University Press.

Soverini, Luca 1998. *Il sofista e l'agora. Sapienti, economia e vita quotidiana nella Grecia classica*. Pisa, Pubblicazioni della Scuola Normale Superiore.

Spatharas, Dimos G. 2001. 'Patterns of Argumentation in Gorgias', *Mnemosyne* 54: 393–408.

Striker, Gisela 1996. 'Methods of Sophistry', in *Essays in Hellenistic Epistemology and Ethics*. Cambridge, Cambridge University Press: 3–21.

Sutton, Dana 1981. 'Critias and Atheism', *CQ* 31: 33–8.

Tell, Håkan 2011. *Plato's Counterfeit Sophists*. Washington, DC: Center for Hellenic Studies.

Thomas, Rosalind 2003. 'Prose Performance Texts: Epideixis and Written Publication in the Late Fifth and Early Fourth Centuries', in H. Yunis (ed.), *Written Texts and the Rise of Literate Culture in Ancient Greece*. Cambridge, Cambridge University Press: 162–88.

Tinsdale, Christopher W. 2010. *Reason's Dark Champions. Constructive Strategies of Sophistic Argument*. Columbia, SC, University of South Carolina Press.

Tordesillas, Alonso 1986. 'L'instance temporelle dans l'argumentation de la première et de la seconde sophistique: la notion de *kairos*', in B. Cassin (ed.), *Le plaisir de parler*. Paris, Les éditions de minuit: 31–61.

——— 2004. 'Synonymique, éthique, philosophie (note sur Prodicos de Ceos)', in J.-P. Cometti (ed.), *L'éthique de la philosophie*. Paris, Éditions Kimé: 55–75.

——— 2008. 'Gorgias et la question de la responsabilité d'Hélène', in F. Alesse et al. (eds.), *Anthropine sophia. Studi di filologia e storiografia filosofica in memoria di Gabriele Giannantoni*. Naples, Bibliopolis: 45–54.

Tortora, Giuseppe 1985. 'Il senso del *kairos* in Gorgia', *SicGymn* 38: 537–64.

Trabattoni, Franco (ed. and trans.) 2000. *Gorgia – Platone. Parola e ragione*. Milan, Unicopli.

Untersteiner, Mario 1947. 'La storia dell'umanità e la soluzione dell'antitesi *nomos-physis* in Prodico di Ceo', *RSF* 2: 117–22.

——— 1954. *The Sophists*. transl. by K. Freeman. Oxford, Blackwell (first published in Italian 1949).

Vegetti, Mario 1989. *L'etica degli antichi*. Rome and Bari, Laterza.

——— 1998. 'Trasimaco', in M. Vegetti (ed.), *Platone. La Repubblica. Vol. I. Libro I*. Naples, Bibliopolis: 233–56.

——— 2018. 'Antropologie della *pleonexia*: Callicle, Trasimaco e Glaucone in Platone', in *Il potere della verità. Saggi platonici*. Rome, Carocci: 195–210.

Verdenius, Willem J. 1981. 'Gorgias' Theory of Deception', in Kerferd 1981b: 116–28.

Versenyi, Lazslo 1962. 'Protagoras' Man-Measure Fragment', *AJPh* 83: 178–84.

Vitanza, Victor 1997. *Negation, Subjectivity, and the History of Rhetoric*. New York, State University of New York Press.

Vlastos, Gregory 1956. 'Protagoras', in M. Ostwald (trans.) and G. Vlastos (ed.), *Plato. Protagoras*. New York, Bobbs-Merrill Company: vii–xxiv.

Wardy, Robert 1996. *The Birth of Rhetoric. Gorgias, Plato and Their Successors*. London, Routledge.

Wedgwood, Ralph 2017. 'The Coherence of Thrasymachus', *OSAP* 53: 33–63.

White, Stephen A. 1995. 'Thrasymachus the Diplomat', *CPh* 90: 307–27.

Whitmarsh, Tim 2015. *Battling the Gods. Atheism in the Ancient World*. New York, Knopf.

Willink, Charles W. 1983. 'Prodikos, "Meteorosophists" and the "Tantalos" Paradigm', *CQ* 33: 25–33.

Winiarczyk, Marek (ed.) 1981. *Diagorae Melii et Theodori Cyrenaei reliquiae*. Leipzig, Teubner.

——— (ed.) 1990. 'Methodisches zum antiken Atheismus', *RM* 133: 1–15.

——— (ed.) 2016. *Diagoras of Melos. A Contribution to the History of Ancient Atheism*. Berlin, De Gruyter.

Wolfsdorf, David 2008a. 'Hesiod, Prodicus, and the Socratics on Work and Pleasure', in Brad Inwood (ed.), *Oxford Studies in Ancient Philosophy XXXV: Winter 2008*. Oxford, Oxford University Press: 1–18.

——— 2008b. 'Prodicus on the Correctness of Names: The Case of τέρψις, χαρά and εὐφροσύνη', *JHS* 35: 1–18.

Woodruff, Paul 1999. 'Rhetoric and Relativism: Protagoras and Gorgias', in A. A. Long (ed.), *The Cambridge Companion to Early Greek Philosophy*. Cambridge, Cambridge University Press: 290–310.

——— 2004. 'Antiphons, Sophist and Athenian'. *OSAP* 26: 323–36.

——— 2013. '*Euboulia* as the Skill Protagoras Taught', in Ophuijsen, Van Ralte, and Stork 2013: 179–93.

Yunis, Harvey 1997. 'Thrasymachus B1: Discord, Not Diplomacy', *CPh* 92: 58–66.

Zeller, Eduard 1923. *Die Philosophie der Griechen in ihrer geschichtlichen Entwicklung*. Fifth edition, Leipzig, Reisland.

Zilioli, Ugo 2013. 'Protagoras Through Plato and Aristotle: A Case for the Philosophical Significance of Ancient Relativism', in Ophuijsen, Van Ralte and Stork 2013: 233–57.

Index of passages discussed

Note: passages for sophists and other Presocratic philosophers are organized by Diels-Kranz (D.-K.) reference, with the chapter number given at the main heading, e.g. Antiphon (D.-K. 89), and the equivalent Laks-Most (L.-M.) reference, where available, given alongside each passage listed. For further explanation of these references, see foreword, p. v.

For EU product safety concerns, contact us at Calle de José Abascal, 56–1°,
28003 Madrid, Spain or eugpsr@cambridge.org.

www.ingramcontent.com/pod-product-compliance
Ingram Content Group UK Ltd.
Pitfield, Milton Keynes, MK11 3LW, UK
UKHW020807190625
459647UK00032B/2369

* 9 7 8 1 1 0 8 7 0 6 2 1 6 *